CW00400333

FOLENS
Ordnance Survey
WORLD ATLAS

PATRICIA HARRISON STEVE HARRISON

CONTENTS

SKILLS
What is a map? ... 3
Scale ... 4
Symbols and keys ... 5
Using the contents and index ... 6
Distance and direction ... 7
Latitude and longitude ... 8/9
Aerial photography ... 10

BRITISH ISLES
Political ... 11
Physical ... 12
Weather ... 13
Communications ... 14
Southern England ... 15
Northern England ... 16
Issues ... 17
Scotland ... 18
Issues ... 19
South West England & Wales ... 20
Issues ... 21
Ireland ... 22
Issues ... 23
British Isles index ... 24

HISTORICAL
Ancient Greece ... 25
Invaders and Settlers ... 26/27
Tudor and Stuart Times
The Armada ... 28
Exploration and Encounters
1450 to 1550 ... 29
Victorian Britain ... 30
The British Empire ... 31
Ancient Egypt ... 32

THE WORLD
Whose ocean? ... 33

The World
Political ... 34/35
Physical ... 36/37

Europe
Political ... 38
Physical ... 39
Acid rain ... 40
Gasping for air ... 41

Asia
Political ... 42
Physical ... 43
Population growth ... 44
Natural disasters ... 45

Africa
Political ... 46
Physical ... 47
Wildlife at risk ... 48
Advancing deserts ... 49

South America
Political ... 50
Physical ... 51
Tropical rainforests ... 52
City growth ... 53

North America
Political ... 54
Physical ... 55
Water for life ... 56
Tourism ... 57

Australasia
Political ... 58
Physical ... 59

Polar Regions
Antarctica ... 60
The Arctic Circle ... 61

International Time Zones ... 62
World index ... 63/64

ACKNOWLEDGEMENTS

The authors and publishers would like to thank the following for permission to reproduce photographs and other materials:

The Ancient Art & Architecture Collection (25; 27; 32)
Aspect Picture Library Limited (58)
Barnabys Picture Library (55)
Bossu/Sygma (40)
Bruce Coleman Limited (33)
Cleveland County Archaeology Section (10)
The Department of Transport (17)
The Environmental Picture Library (41)
Ford Motor Company Limited (21)
Greater Manchester Metro Limited (17)
The Hutchison Library (50; 51)
The National Portrait Gallery (30)
Picturepoint Limited (56; 57; 58)
Popperfoto Limited (45)
Rex Features Limited (17; 23)
The Robert Harding Picture Library (34; 54)
South American Pictures (52)
Spectrum Colour Library (34; 39; 43; 47; 59)
the Still Moving *picture company* (12)
Still Pictures (49)
Susan Griggs Agency (12; 21; 44; 49)
tapol: The Indonesian Human Rights Campaign (44)
Tony Stone Photolibrary – London (9; 14; 17; 19; 23; 33; 39; 41; 43; 44; 48; 50; 51; 53; 55; 56; 57; 59; 60; 61)
Tropix Photographic Library (47)
USSR PhotoLibrary (43)
The Wales Tourist Board (21)
Wildlife Matters Photographic Library (52)
ZEFA (14; 17; 33; 39; 48; 53)

The publishers have made every effort to contact copyright holders but this has not always been possible. If any have been overlooked we will be pleased to make any necessary arrangements.

To the best of the publishers' knowledge, information in this atlas was correct at the time of going to press. No responsibility can be accepted for any errors.

On pages 11, 12, 13, 14, 15, 16, 18, 20, 22, 26, 27, 28 and 30 of this atlas, mapping of Ireland is based on the Ordnance Survey with the permission of:
1) The Government of the Republic of Ireland (Permit No 5541)
2) The Controller of H.M. Stationery Office (Permit No 460)

Graphics & design: Jillian Luff of Bitmap Graphics.
Artwork: Ann Baum & Peter Dennis of Linda Rogers Associates; Peter Utton of Graham-Cameron Illustration.
Cover design: In-Touch Creative Services Ltd.

First published 1992 by Folens Limited, Dunstable and Dublin, and Ordnance Survey, Southampton.

Folens Limited, Albert House, Apex Business Centre, Boscombe Road, Dunstable, LU5 4RL, England.

	non-net	net
ISBN	1 852 76330 2 (Folens)	1 852 76491 0 (Folens)
ISBN	0 319 00338 8 (OS)	0 319 00298 5 (OS)

Printed by Bath Press Colourbooks.

What is a map?

Maps have been used since
prehistoric times. They help us
understand the world around us.

map is a way of passing information.

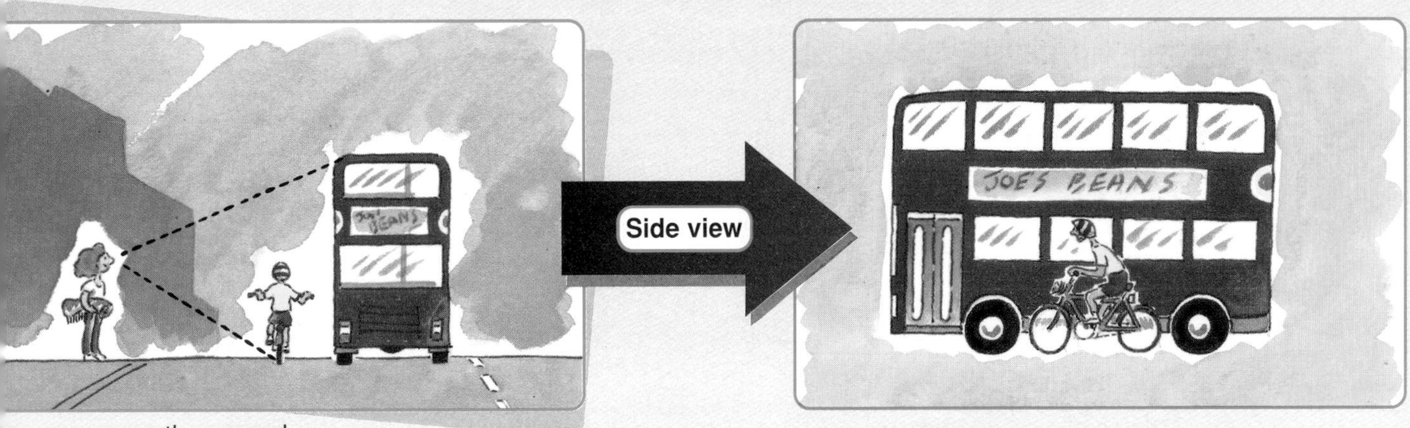

Side view
JOE'S BEANS

en we are on the ground
see the world from a side view.

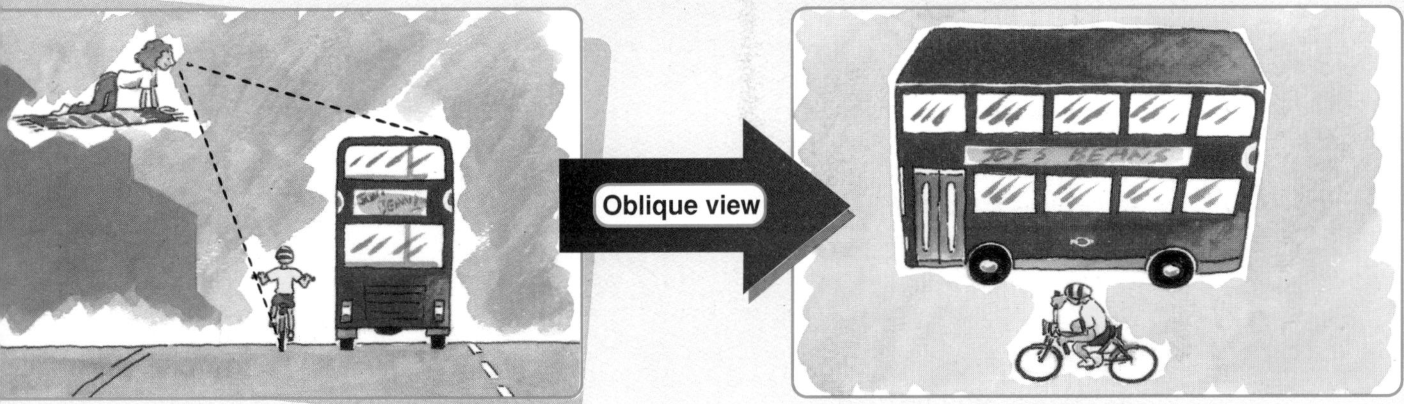

Oblique view
JOE'S BEANS

ve fly on a magic carpet the world
ks different. This is an oblique view.

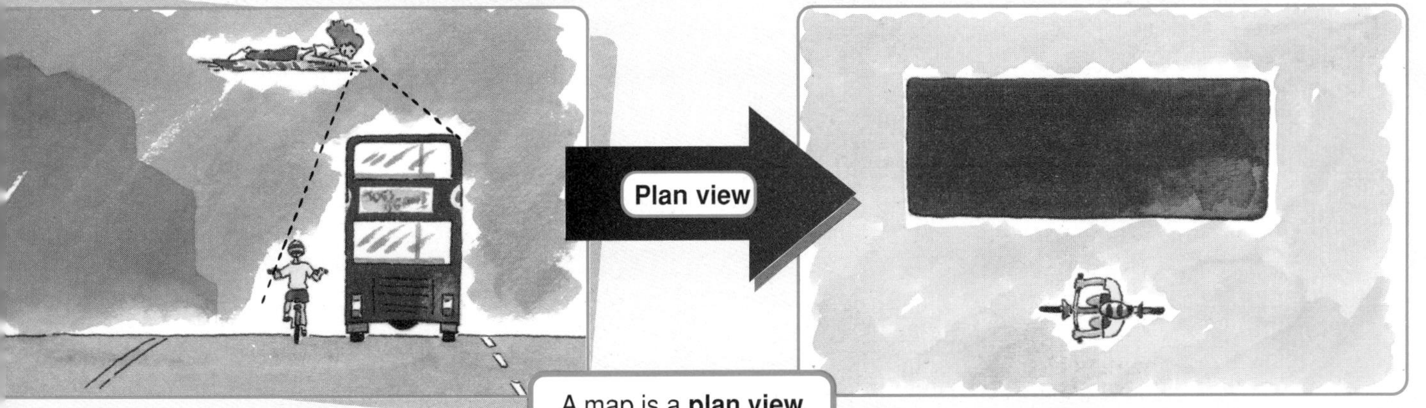

Plan view

ve fly above the objects they look
erent again. This is a plan view.

A map is a **plan view**.
It is a view from above.

Scale

The higher you are, the more area you can see.

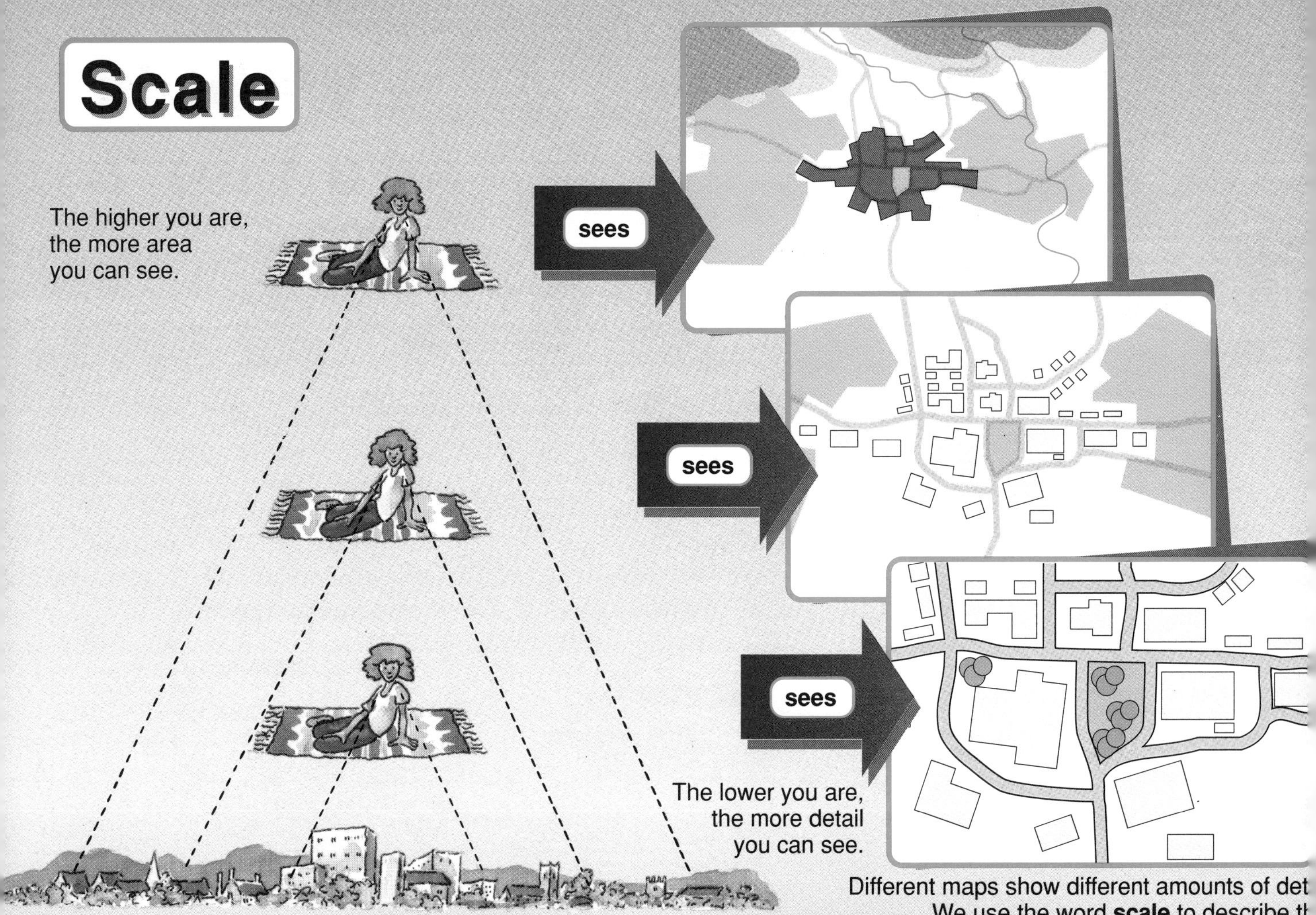

sees

sees

sees

The lower you are, the more detail you can see.

Different maps show different amounts of det
We use the word **scale** to describe tl

A builder needs a **large scale map** which shows the detail of roads, pavements and buildings.

A lorry driver need: much **smaller scale m** which gives informati about main roa between tow

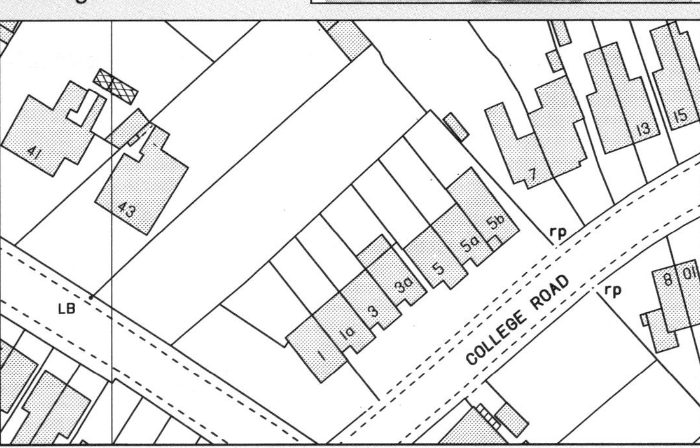

41
43
13
15
7
5b
5a
5
3a
3
1a
1
rp
rp
8
LB
COLLEGE ROAD

This map would be no use to the lorry driver.

Crawley
Worthy Down
Kings Worthy
M3
Grange
Old Alresford
New Alresfo
Itchen Abbas
Itchen Stoke
Littleton
A34
Headbourne Worthy
B3047
Easton
Ovington
WINCHESTER
VENTA
A31
Tichborne
B3046
Cheriton
New Cheriton
South Downs Way
A272
Chilcomb
A3090
Oliver's Battery
ROMAN ROAD
A33
Longwood Warren
Morestead
Compton
Kilmeston

This map would be no use to the builder.

Choosing the right scale of map is important.

Example:
1 cm on the map stands for 1250 cm on the ground.

0 25 m
Scale 1:1250

Maps show the scale in a scale box.

Symbols and keys

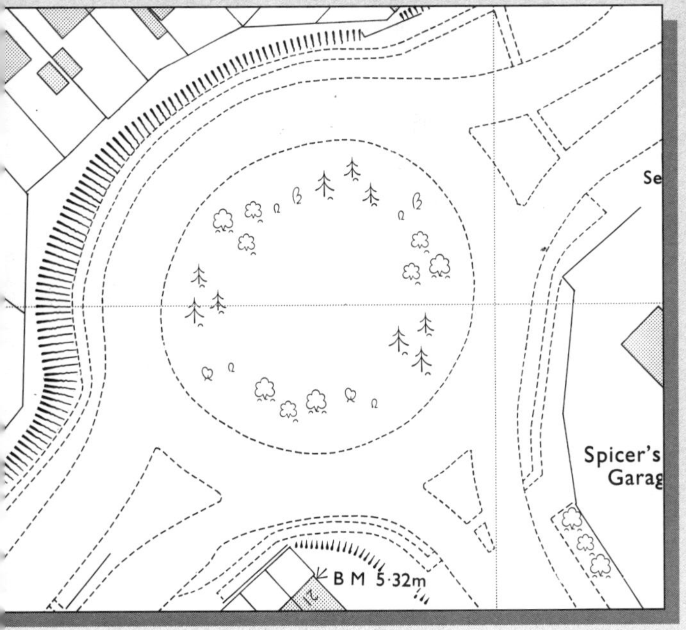
Se
Spicer's
Garag
B M 5·32m

When using a large scale map we often know what is shown by its shape. Features such as traffic roundabouts, churches, running tracks and docks are easy to recognise from their shape.

Other features are not so easy to recognise. Many buildings have the same shape. In order to show which building is a post office and which is a public house, the map maker uses letter symbols.

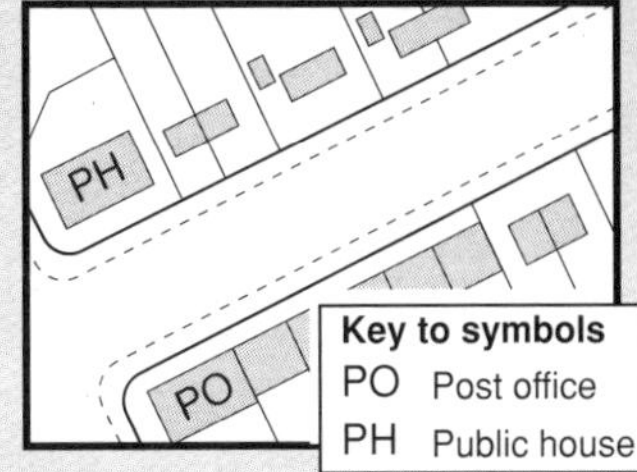
PH
PO
Key to symbols
PO Post office
PH Public house

me maps have word, letter and picture symbols to help us derstand what is shown.

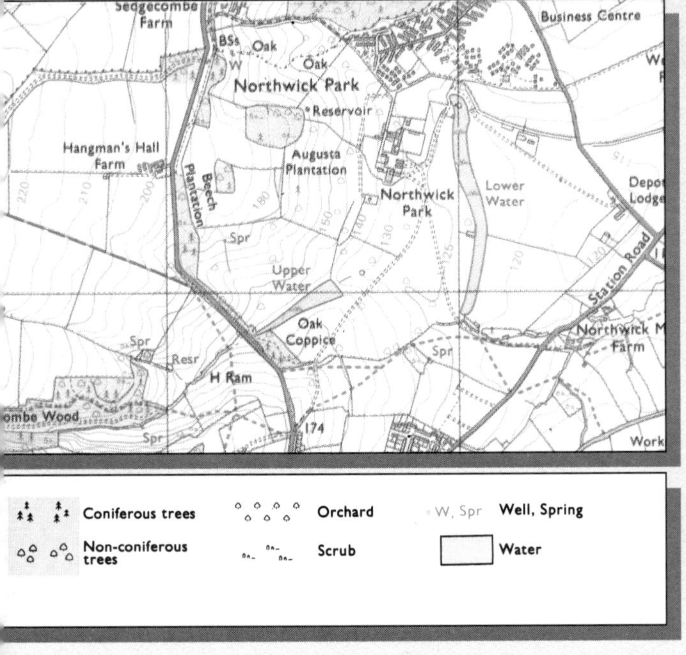
Sedgecombe Farm
Business Centre
Oak
Northwick Park
Reservoir
Hangman's Hall Farm
Augusta Plantation
Beech Plantation
Northwick Park
Lower Water
Depot Lodge
Spr
Upper Water
Station Road
Oak Coppice
Northwick M Farm
Spr
Resr
H Ram
ombe Wood
174
Work
Coniferous trees
Non-coniferous trees
Orchard
Scrub
W, Spr
Well, Spring
Water

Map makers also use different colours to make the maps easy to follow.

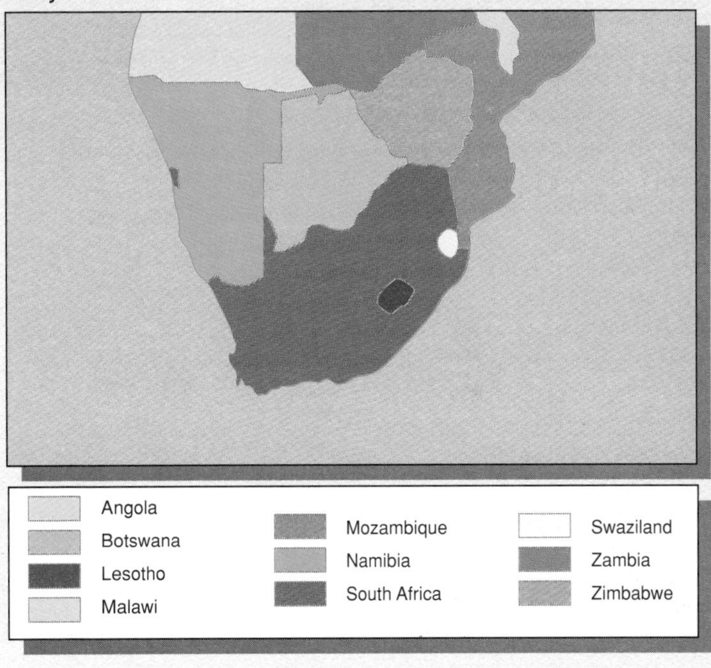
Angola
Botswana
Lesotho
Malawi
Mozambique
Namibia
South Africa
Swaziland
Zambia
Zimbabwe

Map keys

When symbols and colours are used in a map they are usually shown in a key.

The key explains the meaning of the symbols and colours.

The maps in this atlas have their own keys. Read the keys to help you understand the maps.

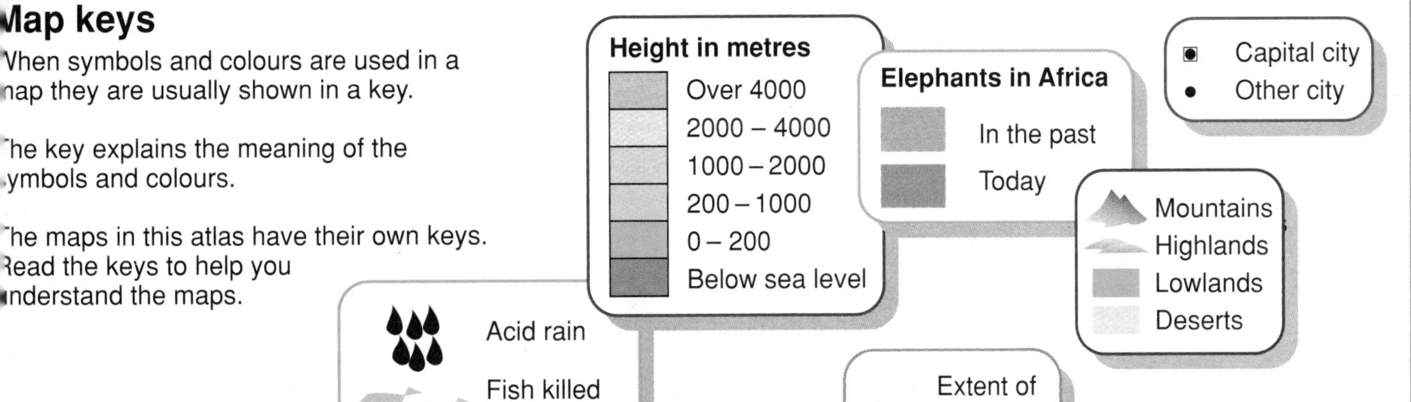
Height in metres
Over 4000
2000 – 4000
1000 – 2000
200 – 1000
0 – 200
Below sea level
Elephants in Africa
In the past
Today
Capital city
Other city
Mountains
Highlands
Lowlands
Deserts
Acid rain
Fish killed by pollution
Extent of frozen ice
Air route

Using the contents and index

An atlas is a book of maps.

Contents

If you want to find out about a continent or a theme you should first look at the contents page at the front of this atlas.
For example: If you are interested in the mountains and rivers of South America you would look for **South America, Physical** in the contents.

Africa 46
Political 47
Physical 48
Wildlife at risk 48
Advancing deserts 49

South America 50
Political 51
Physical 51
Tropical rainforests 52
City growth 53

Physical maps tell us about the mountains, rivers and lakes of areas.
Political maps tell us about countries, cities and population.

C
Cairo Egypt 46 D6
CAMBODIA Asia 42 E3
CAMEROON Africa 46 C4
CANADA North America 54 C4
Canary Islands Atlantic Ocean 47 G6

name — page number
Cairo Egypt **46 D6**
country — position on page

Index

If you want to find a place such as a river or a city, turn instead to the index at the back of the atlas. Places are listed alphabetically in the index.
For example: If you want to find out about Cairo look under the '**C**' section of the index.

Some places appear on a number of maps in this atlas, eg London. They are listed in the index under the page on which they appear at the largest scale.

Grid references

Most pages have a grid around the edge of the map. The horizontal axis is marked in letters A, B, C, etc. The vertical axis is marked in numbers 1, 2, 3, etc. Using grid references helps us locate places quickly. Cairo can easily be found in grid square **D6**.

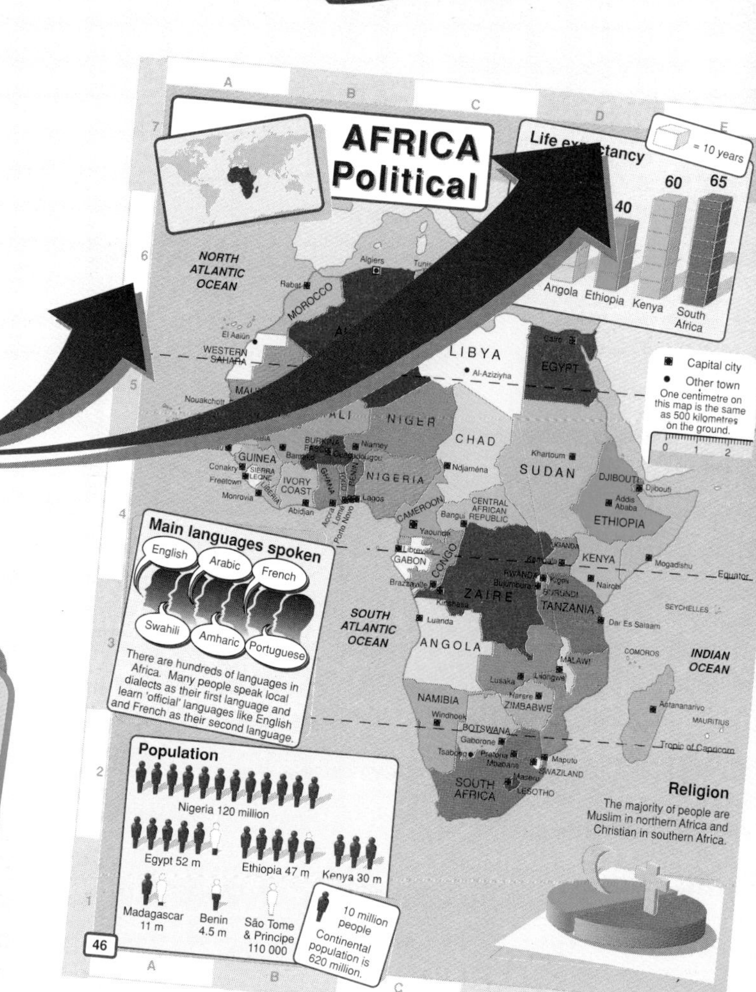

AFRICA
Political
Life expectancy
= 10 years
40
60
65
Angola
Ethiopia
Kenya
South Africa
NORTH ATLANTIC OCEAN
MOROCCO
WESTERN SAHARA
LIBYA
EGYPT
NIGER
CHAD
SUDAN
NIGERIA
DJIBOUTI
ETHIOPIA
KENYA
TANZANIA
ZAIRE
ANGOLA
NAMIBIA
ZIMBABWE
BOTSWANA
SOUTH AFRICA
SOUTH ATLANTIC OCEAN
INDIAN OCEAN
Capital city
Other town
One centimetre on this map is the same as 500 kilometres on the ground.
Equator
Tropic of Capricorn
Main languages spoken
English
Arabic
French
Swahili
Amharic
Portuguese
There are hundreds of languages in Africa. Many people speak local dialects as their first language and learn 'official' languages like English and French as their second language.
Population
Nigeria 120 million
Egypt 52 m
Ethiopia 47 m
Kenya 30 m
Madagascar 11 m
Benin 4.5 m
São Tome & Principe 110 000
10 million people
Continental population is 620 million.
Religion
The majority of people are Muslim in northern Africa and Christian in southern Africa.
46

Use your skills

Turn to the contents.
On which page will you find:
a) The mountains of Asia?
b) The cities of Africa?
c) The countries of South America?
d) The rivers of Europe?

Turn to the index.
What is the page number and grid reference for:
Dar es Salaam, Berlin, Lima, Washington and Tokyo?
These are the capital cities of which countries?

Distance and direction

ps can tell us how far one place is from another. To check
:ances we must use the map's scale line.

'ind the distance from Abergavenny to Monmouth, place
r ruler on the map and measure the distance between the
town centres.

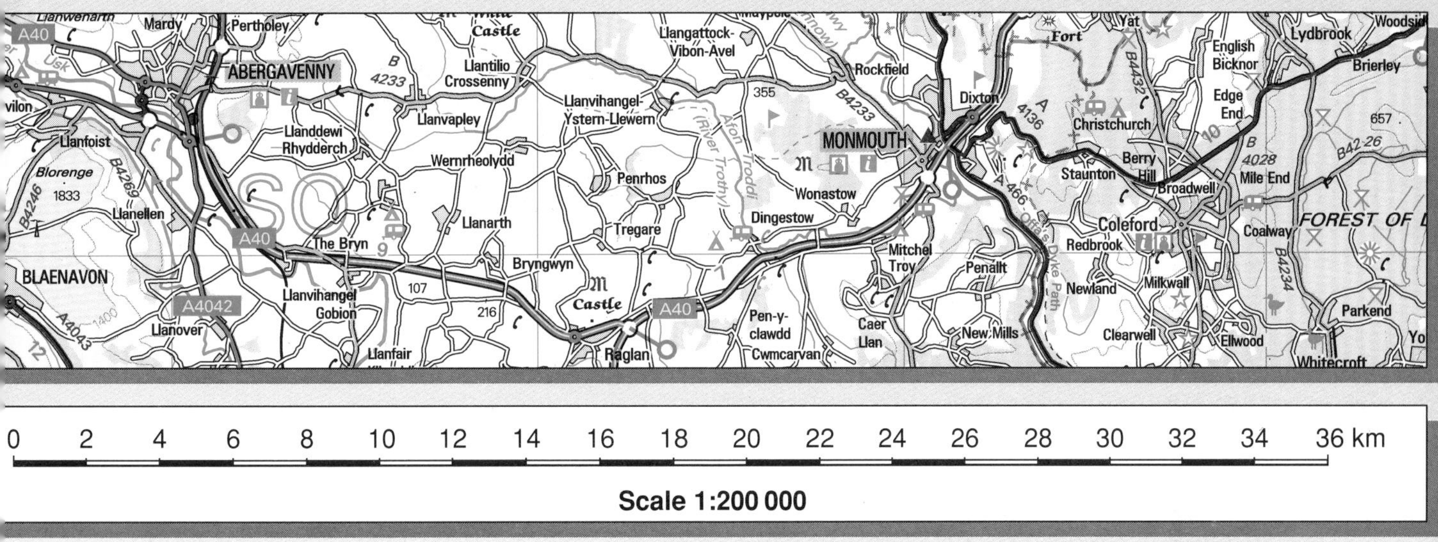

ABERGAVENNY
MONMOUTH
BLAENAVON
Mardy
Pertholey
Castle
Llantilio Crossenny
Llangattock-Vibon-Avel
Rockfield
Dixton
Fort
Yat
English Bicknor
Lydbrook
Brierley
Llanfoist
Blorenge
1833
Llanddewi Rhydderch
Llanvapley
Llanvihangel-Ystern-Llewern
Wernrheolydd
Penrhos
Wonastow
Dingestow
Christchurch
Berry Hill
Staunton
Broadwell
Edge End
Mile End
Coleford
Redbrook
Coalway
FOREST OF
Llanellen
Llanarth
Tregare
The Bryn
Bryngwyn
Mitchel Troy
Penallt
Newland
Milkwall
Llanvihangel Gobion
Llanover
Llanfair
Raglan
Pen-y-clawdd
Cwmcarvan
Caer Llan
New Mills
Clearwell
Ellwood
Parkend
Whitecroft
A40
A4042
A4043
B4233
B4269
B4246
B4432
B4228
B4234
A466
A4136
Offa's Dyke Path
River Trothy
Afon Troddi
355
107
216
657
0 2 4 6 8 10 12 14 16 18 20 22 24 26 28 30 32 34 36 km
Scale 1:200 000

ıeasures 10 cm. Check this distance on the scale line. 10 cm is 20 km on the ground. So we know that Abergavenny is
km from Monmouth.

ɔple do not usually travel in straight lines. A better way to measure the distance is to use string. This allows you to follow the
ds as they twist and turn. Using string, measure the distance between Abergavenny and Monmouth (a) on the B4233 and
on the A40. Which route is longer and by how much?

ıtinental maps are at a much smaller scale. Use your ruler
scale line to find the distance between Brasilia and La
:.

BRAZIL
La Paz
BOLIVIA
Brasilia
N
NW
NE
W
E
SW
SE
S

0 1000 2000 3000 km

Scale 1:50 000 000

As well as knowing the distance between places we should also know the direction.
By using the 8-point compass we can see that La Paz is west of Brasilia.

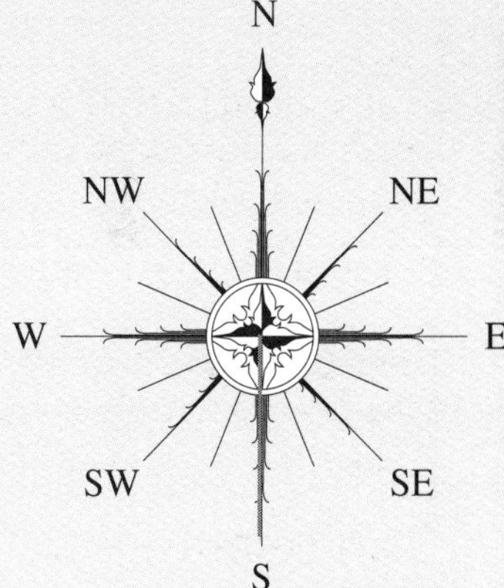

N
NW
NE
W
E
SW
SE
S

Use your skills

Use the political map of South America on page 50 to find these distances and directions.

Copy and complete the chart. (Distances in km.)

From	To	Distance	Direction
Buenos Aires	Falkland Is		
Montevideo	Buenos Aires		
Santiago	Brasilia		
Montevideo	Lima		
Caracas	Bogota		
La Paz	Caracas		

Latitude and longitude

The world maps in this atlas have a grid reference system which is used all around the world. The earth has had imaginary lines drawn on it to help people locate places.

Latitude

Lines drawn horizontally around the earth are called **lines of latitude**. The first line drawn is where the earth's circumference is greatest. This line is called the **equator**.

Parallel lines are drawn every 15° north and south of the equator (0°). The north pole is at 90° north and the south pole is at 90° south. Lines in between are described as degrees north and south of the equator.

The lines of latitude are then transferred on to a flat map.

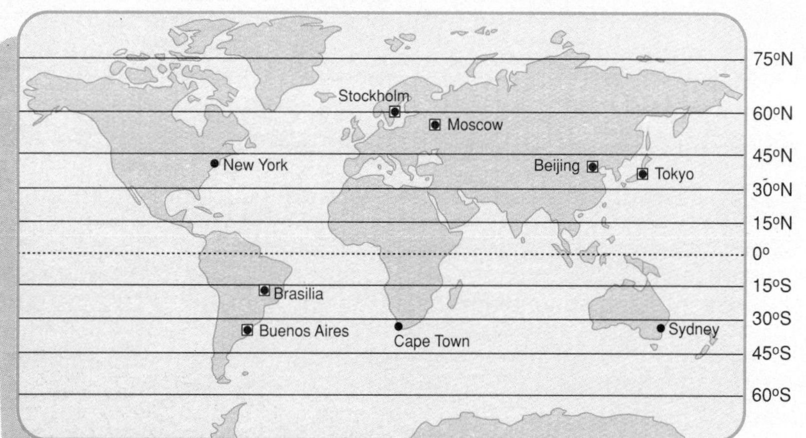

75°N
60°N
45°N
30°N
15°N
0°
15°S
30°S
45°S
60°S
Stockholm
Moscow
New York
Beijing
Tokyo
Brasilia
Buenos Aires
Cape Town
Sydney

Use your skills

At what line of latitude is (a) Stockholm (b) Brasilia?

Name three cities between latitude 30° south and 45° south.

Between which two lines of latitude is (a) New York (b) Tokyo (c) Moscow (d) Beijing?

Longitude

Lines drawn vertically round the earth are called **lines of longitude**. The first line drawn is called the prime meridian. It runs through Greenwich, London.

The prime meridian was chosen in 1884 because there was a need for all sailors to use the same system and in those days Britain's navy was the largest in the world.

Other lines of longitude are drawn every 15° east and west of the prime meridian (0°) until they meet at 180°, close to New Zealand.

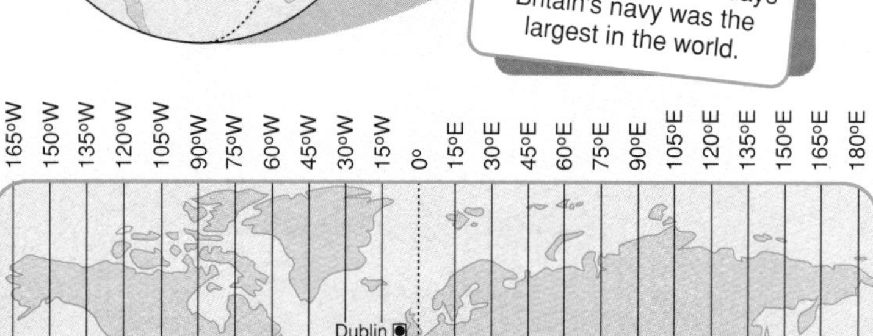

165°W
150°W
135°W
120°W
105°W
90°W
75°W
60°W
45°W
30°W
15°W
0°
15°E
30°E
45°E
60°E
75°E
90°E
105°E
120°E
135°E
150°E
165°E
180°E
Dublin
Madrid
Rabat
Alexandria
Dhaka
Bombay
Bogota
Perth
Falkland Is

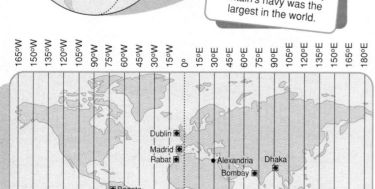

The lines of longitude are then transferred on to a flat map.

Use your skills

On which line of longitude are (a) the Falkland Islands (b) Alexandria (c) Dhaka?

Between which two lines of longitude are Dublin, Madrid and Rabat?

Between which two lines of longitude is (a) Bombay (b) Perth (c) Bogota?

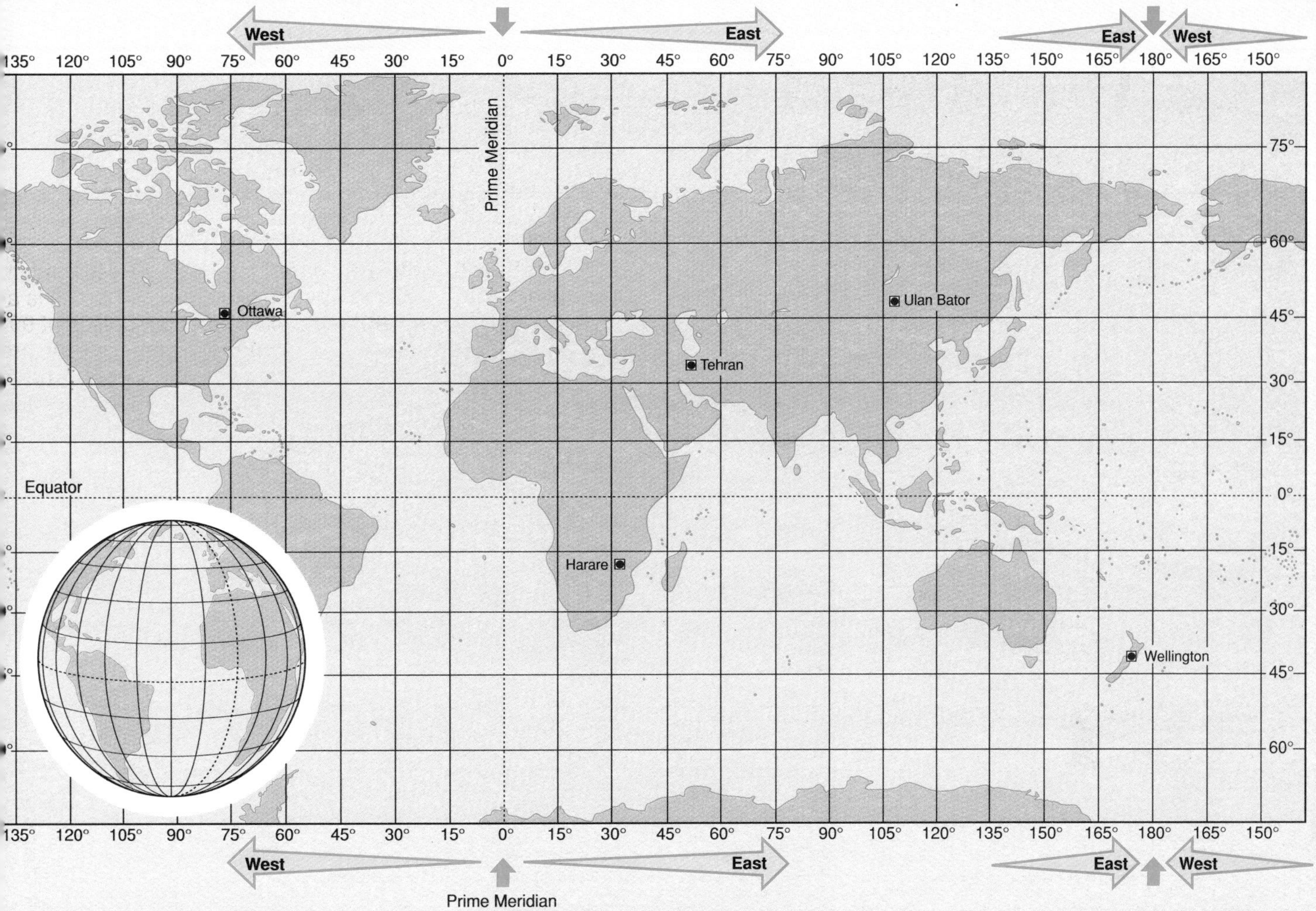

West | East | East | West

135° 120° 105° 90° 75° 60° 45° 30° 15° 0° 15° 30° 45° 60° 75° 90° 105° 120° 135° 150° 165° 180° 165° 150°

Prime Meridian

75° 60° 45° 30° 15° 0° 15° 30° 45° 60°

Equator

Ottawa

Ulan Bator

Tehran

Harare

Wellington

135° 120° 105° 90° 75° 60° 45° 30° 15° 0° 15° 30° 45° 60° 75° 90° 105° 120° 135° 150° 165° 180° 165° 150°

West | East | East | West

Prime Meridian

ɛ lines of latitude and longitude are now nbined on a flat map. Any place in the rld can be located using two reference nts, eg Ottawa is at 45° north of the ıator and 75° west of the prime meridian. write this - 45°N 75°W.

Use your skills

Which cities are located at these points?

(a) 17°S 31°E
(b) 35°N 51°E
(c) 41°S 174°E
(d) 47°N 106°E

During the year the earth tilts as it circles the sun. In June the sun's rays are stronger in the northern half (hemisphere) of the earth. The Tropic of Cancer is an imaginary line marking the point where the sun is overhead on June 21st.

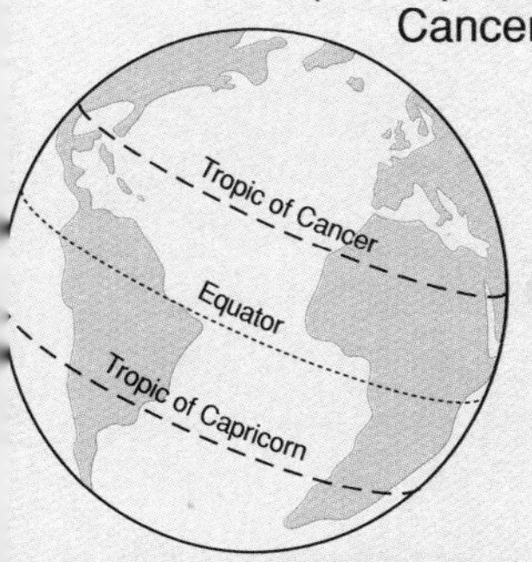

Tropic of Cancer

Equator

Tropic of Capricorn

Sun's rays June 21st

The Tropic of Capricorn marks the point where the sun is overhead on December 21st.

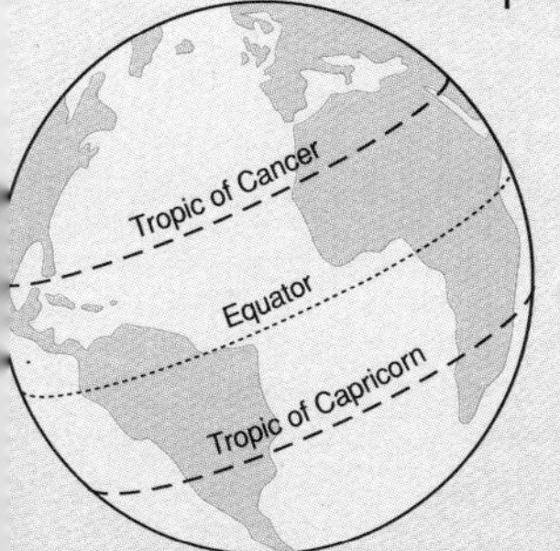

Tropic of Cancer

Equator

Tropic of Capricorn

Sun's rays December 21st

There is a strong link between latitude and climate. High latitudes (polar climate) have very low temperatures all year round. Low latitudes (equatorial climate) have hot, wet weather all year round.

Aerial photography

Aerial photographs when used with maps provide us with a great deal of information. Look at the photograph for physical features such as rivers or hills and then find them on the map.

Aerial photographs give us information which is not found on maps.

Aerial photograph

Use your skills

1. What is the highest building?
2. How is the railway supported?
3. What is the weather like?
4. What season is it?
5. What is growing in the fields?

Maps give us information which is not found on aerial photographs.

Ordnance Survey map extract

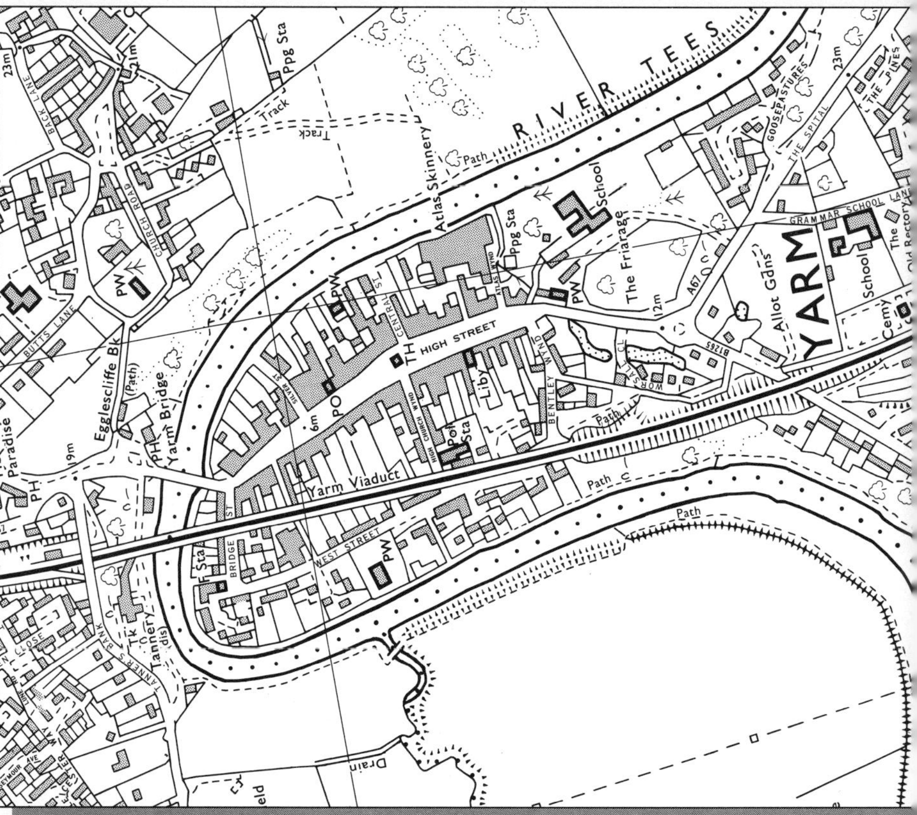

RIVER TEES
YARM
Yarm Viaduct
HIGH STREET
WEST STREET
Yarm Bridge
Egglescliffe Bk
Atlas Skinnery
The Friarage
School
Allot Gdns
Cemy
PW
PO
Liby
Pol Sta
Ppg Sta
Path
Track
Drain
Paradise
BUTTS LANE
CHURCH ROAD
BACK LANE
BENTLEY WYND
GRAMMAR SCHOOL LANE
THE SPITAL
GOOSEPASTURES
Tannery (dis)
A67
B1265
23m
21m
12m
9m
6m

Use your skills

1. What is this place called?
2. What is the main street called?
3. How many post offices are there?
4. Name the road which passes under the railway bridge.
5. Give the address of a Post Office.

The map has been turned so that it matches the photograph above as closely as possible.

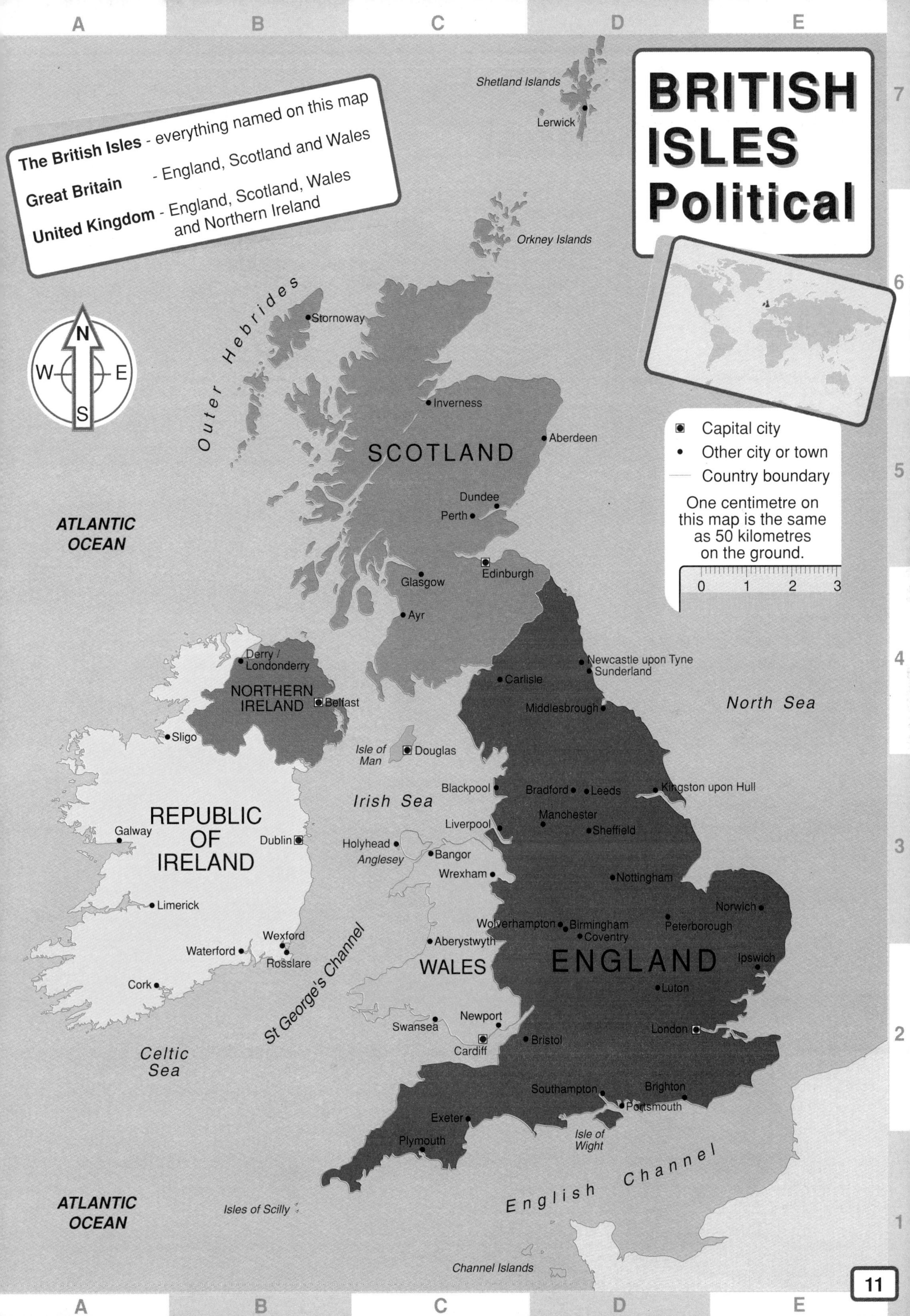

BRITISH ISLES Political
The British Isles - everything named on this map
Great Britain - England, Scotland and Wales
United Kingdom - England, Scotland, Wales and Northern Ireland
Capital city
Other city or town
Country boundary
One centimetre on this map is the same as 50 kilometres on the ground.
0 1 2 3
N
S
W
E
A B C D E
1 2 3 4 5 6 7
Shetland Islands
Lerwick
Orkney Islands
Outer Hebrides
Stornoway
Inverness
Aberdeen
SCOTLAND
Dundee
Perth
Edinburgh
Glasgow
Ayr
ATLANTIC OCEAN
Derry / Londonderry
NORTHERN IRELAND
Belfast
Sligo
Isle of Man
Douglas
Newcastle upon Tyne
Sunderland
Carlisle
Middlesbrough
North Sea
Blackpool
Bradford
Leeds
Kingston upon Hull
Irish Sea
REPUBLIC OF IRELAND
Galway
Dublin
Holyhead
Anglesey
Bangor
Liverpool
Manchester
Sheffield
Wrexham
Nottingham
Limerick
Norwich
Wolverhampton
Birmingham
Coventry
Peterborough
Wexford
Waterford
Rosslare
Aberystwyth
WALES
ENGLAND
Ipswich
Cork
St George's Channel
Luton
Newport
Swansea
Cardiff
Bristol
London
Celtic Sea
Southampton
Brighton
Portsmouth
Exeter
Isle of Wight
Plymouth
English Channel
ATLANTIC OCEAN
Isles of Scilly
Channel Islands

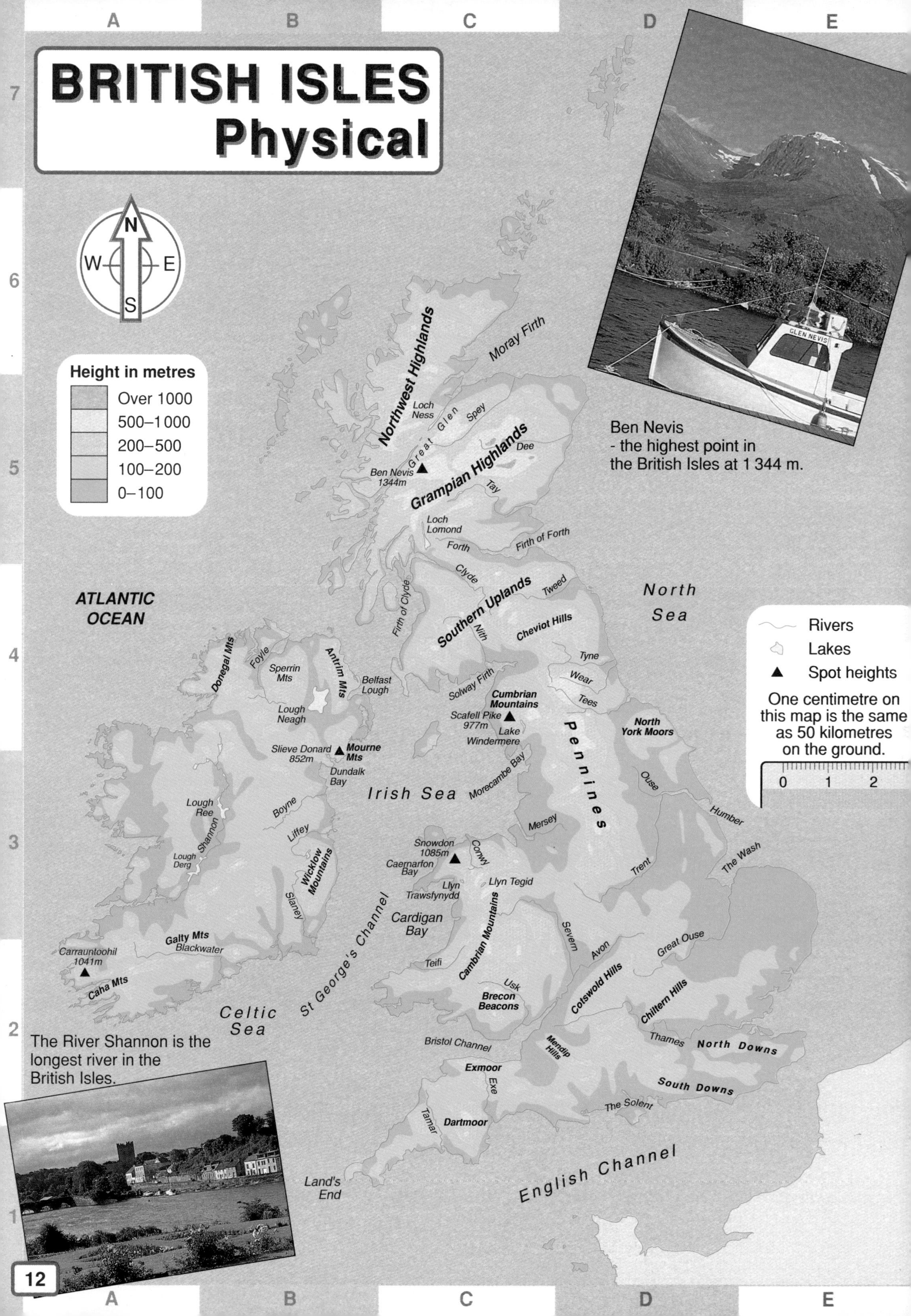
A
B
C
D
E
7
6
5
4
3
2
1
BRITISH ISLES
Physical
N
W
E
S
Height in metres
Over 1000
500–1 000
200–500
100–200
0–100
Northwest Highlands
Moray Firth
Loch Ness
Great Glen
Spey
Grampian Highlands
Dee
Ben Nevis 1344m
Tay
Loch Lomond
Forth
Firth of Forth
Clyde
Tweed
Southern Uplands
Firth of Clyde
Nith
Cheviot Hills
ATLANTIC OCEAN
North Sea
Donegal Mts
Foyle
Sperrin Mts
Antrim Mts
Belfast Lough
Lough Neagh
Solway Firth
Cumbrian Mountains
Tyne
Wear
Tees
Scafell Pike 977m
Lake Windermere
North York Moors
Pennines
Slieve Donard 852m
Mourne Mts
Dundalk Bay
Irish Sea
Morecambe Bay
Ouse
Humber
Lough Ree
Shannon
Boyne
Liffey
Lough Derg
Wicklow Mountains
Mersey
Snowdon 1085m
Conwy
Caernarfon Bay
Llyn Tegid
Llyn Trawsfynydd
Trent
The Wash
Slaney
St George's Channel
Cardigan Bay
Cambrian Mountains
Severn
Avon
Great Ouse
Galty Mts
Blackwater
Carrauntoohil 1041m
Caha Mts
Teifi
Usk
Brecon Beacons
Cotswold Hills
Chiltern Hills
Celtic Sea
Bristol Channel
Mendip Hills
Thames
North Downs
Exmoor
Exe
South Downs
The Solent
Tamar
Dartmoor
Land's End
English Channel
Rivers
Lakes
Spot heights
One centimetre on this map is the same as 50 kilometres on the ground.
0
1
2
GLEN NEVIS

Ben Nevis
- the highest point in the British Isles at 1 344 m.

The River Shannon is the longest river in the British Isles.

BRITISH ISLES Weather

e British Isles are in the path of winds which blow across the Atlantic Ocean. These winds are mid-way between warm, moist air from the south and cold dry air from the north. This mixture gives us our very changeable weather.

As the clouds reach the land they start to drop rain. When the clouds rise above high ground they cool and drop even more rain. The west of the British Isles is very wet because the clouds arrive there first. Compare the physical map opposite with the rainfall map. Can you see a connection between high land and heavy rainfall?

rain
rising
air cools;
drops
moisture
rain
shadow
ind picks up
moisture
over the sea

Rainfall

(mm)

- More than 1800
- 1200 - 1800
- 800 - 1200
- 600 - 800
- 0 - 600

anuary temperatures

winter, temperatures in the British les are lower in the east than in e west, although mountain eas are the coldest of all.

mperature (°C)

- More than 7°
- 6° - 7°
- 5° - 6°
- 4° - 5°
- 3° - 4°
- Less than 3°

July temperatures

In summer, temperatures are lower in the north than in the south.

Temperature (°C)

- More than 17°
- 16° - 17°
- 15° - 16°
- 14° - 15°
- 13° - 14°
- Less than 13°

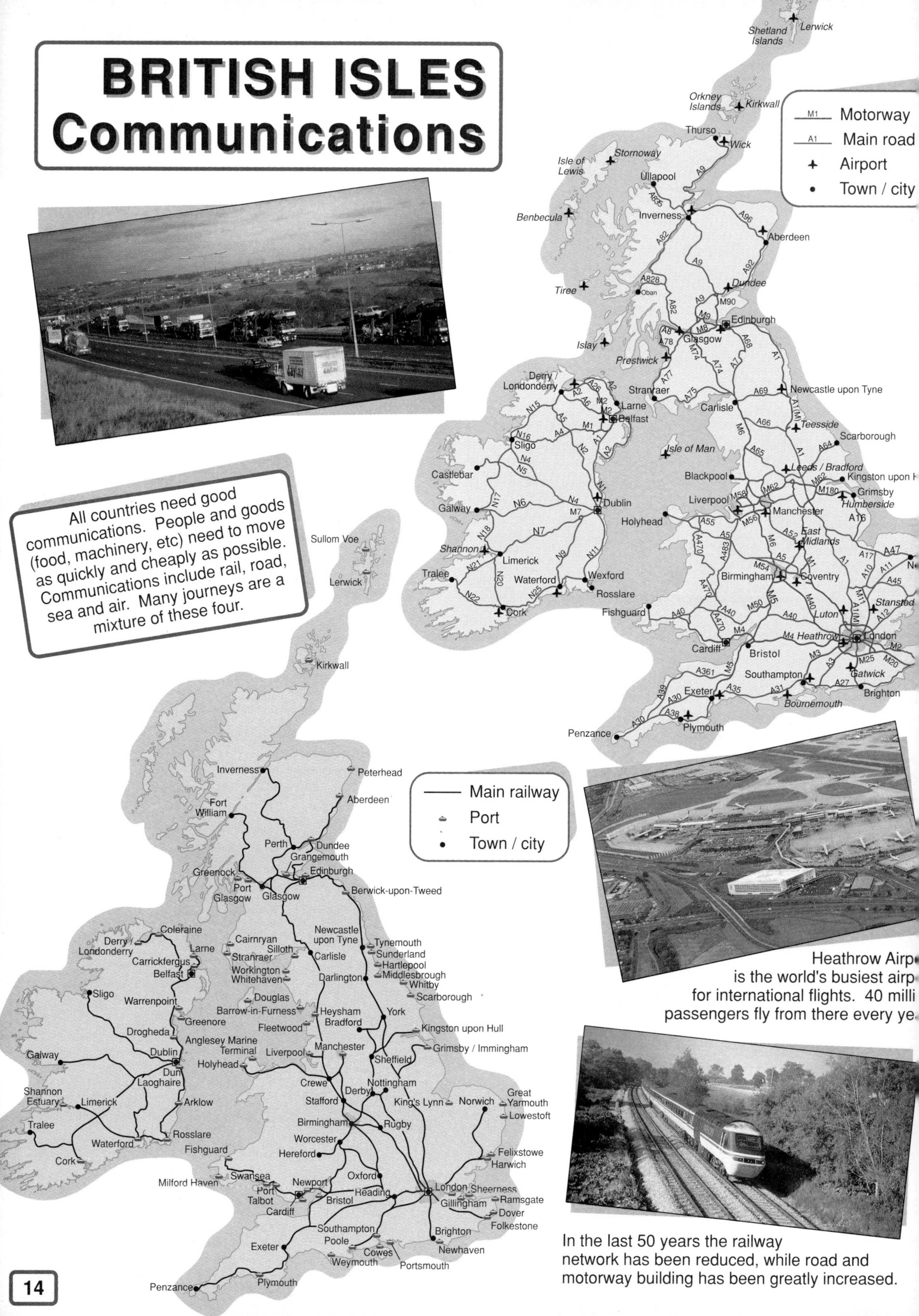

BRITISH ISLES
Communications
All countries need good communications. People and goods (food, machinery, etc) need to move as quickly and cheaply as possible. Communications include rail, road, sea and air. Many journeys are a mixture of these four.
M1 Motorway
A1 Main road
Airport
Town / city
Shetland Islands
Lerwick
Orkney Islands
Kirkwall
Thurso
Wick
Isle of Lewis
Stornoway
Ullapool
Benbecula
Inverness
Aberdeen
Tiree
Oban
Dundee
Edinburgh
Glasgow
Islay
Prestwick
Derry / Londonderry
Stranraer
Larne
Belfast
Newcastle upon Tyne
Carlisle
Teesside
Sligo
Isle of Man
Scarborough
Castlebar
Leeds / Bradford
Blackpool
Kingston upon H
Grimsby
Humberside
Galway
Dublin
Liverpool
Manchester
Holyhead
East Midlands
Shannon
Limerick
Tralee
Waterford
Wexford
Rosslare
Birmingham
Coventry
Cork
Fishguard
Luton
Stansted
Heathrow
London
Cardiff
Bristol
Southampton
Gatwick
Exeter
Bournemouth
Brighton
Plymouth
Penzance
Main railway
Port
Town / city
Sullom Voe
Peterhead
Fort William
Perth
Grangemouth
Greenock
Port Glasgow
Berwick-upon-Tweed
Coleraine
Cairnryan
Silloth
Tynemouth
Sunderland
Hartlepool
Middlesbrough
Whitby
Carrickfergus
Workington
Whitehaven
Darlington
Warrenpoint
Douglas
Barrow-in-Furness
Heysham
York
Greenore
Drogheda
Fleetwood
Kingston upon Hull
Anglesey Marine Terminal
Grimsby / Immingham
Sheffield
Dun Laoghaire
Crewe
Nottingham
Derby
Shannon Estuary
Arklow
Stafford
King's Lynn
Norwich
Great Yarmouth
Lowestoft
Rugby
Worcester
Hereford
Felixstowe
Harwich
Milford Haven
Swansea
Port Talbot
Newport
Oxford
Reading
Sheerness
Ramsgate
Gillingham
Dover
Folkestone
Poole
Cowes
Weymouth
Portsmouth
Newhaven
Heathrow Airp
is the world's busiest airp
for international flights. 40 milli
passengers fly from there every ye
In the last 50 years the railway network has been reduced, while road and motorway building has been greatly increased.
14

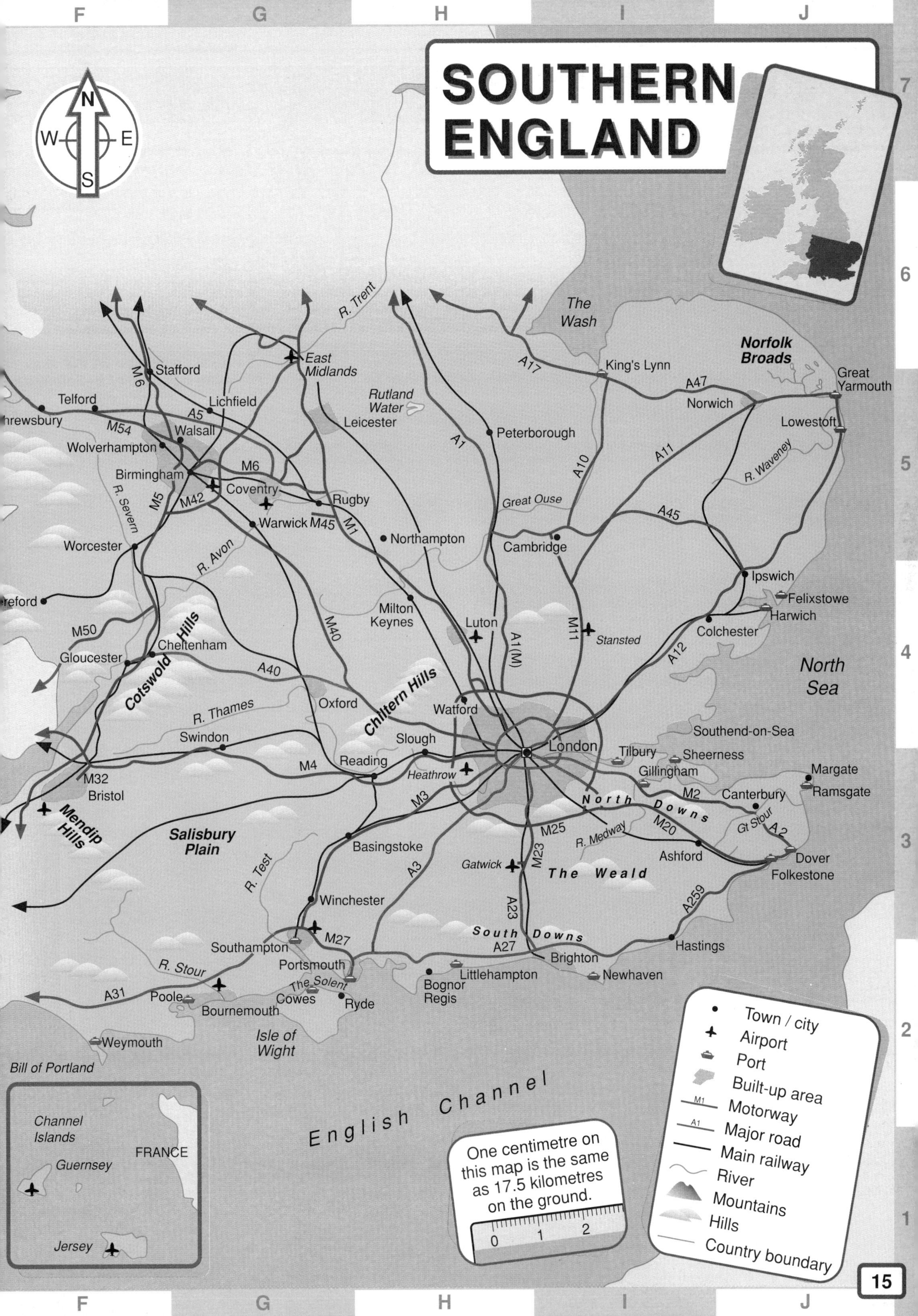
SOUTHERN ENGLAND
N
W
E
S
F
G
H
I
J
7
6
5
4
3
2
1
The Wash
Norfolk Broads
King's Lynn
Great Yarmouth
Norwich
Lowestoft
R. Waveney
A47
A17
A11
A10
A45
A1
R. Trent
East Midlands
Rutland Water
Leicester
Peterborough
Stafford
Lichfield
Telford
Shrewsbury
Walsall
Wolverhampton
Birmingham
Coventry
Rugby
Warwick
Northampton
M6
M54
A5
M42
M5
M45
M1
R. Severn
Worcester
R. Avon
Great Ouse
Cambridge
Ipswich
Felixstowe
Harwich
Colchester
Hereford
M50
Gloucester
Cheltenham
Cotswold Hills
Milton Keynes
Luton
M40
A1(M)
M11
Stansted
A12
North Sea
A40
Oxford
Chiltern Hills
Watford
R. Thames
Swindon
Slough
London
Southend-on-Sea
Tilbury
Sheerness
Gillingham
Margate
Ramsgate
M32
Bristol
M4
Reading
Heathrow
Canterbury
M2
North Downs
Mendip Hills
Salisbury Plain
M3
M25
R. Medway
M20
Gt Stour
A2
Basingstoke
Ashford
Dover
Folkestone
R. Test
A3
Gatwick
M23
The Weald
Winchester
A23
A259
South Downs
A27
M27
Southampton
Hastings
Brighton
Newhaven
R. Stour
Portsmouth
Littlehampton
The Solent
Bognor Regis
A31
Poole
Cowes
Ryde
Bournemouth
Isle of Wight
Weymouth
Bill of Portland
English Channel
Channel Islands
FRANCE
Guernsey
Jersey
One centimetre on this map is the same as 17.5 kilometres on the ground.
0
1
2
Town / city
Airport
Port
Built-up area
M1
Motorway
A1
Major road
Main railway
River
Mountains
Hills
Country boundary

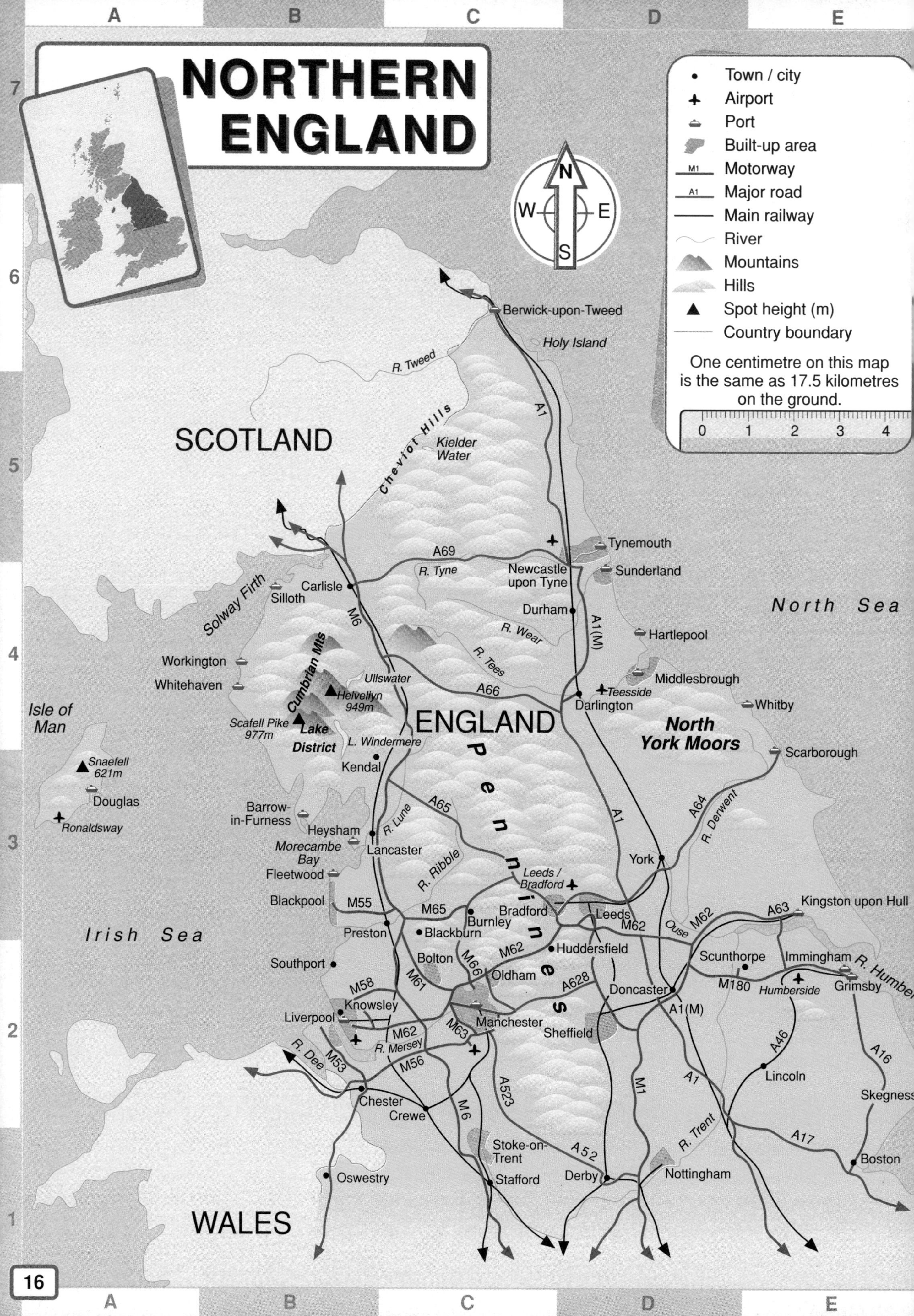

NORTHERN ENGLAND
Town / city
Airport
Port
Built-up area
Motorway
Major road
Main railway
River
Mountains
Hills
Spot height (m)
Country boundary
One centimetre on this map is the same as 17.5 kilometres on the ground.
0 1 2 3 4
N
S
E
W
A B C D E
7 6 5 4 3 2 1
SCOTLAND
ENGLAND
WALES
Isle of Man
North Sea
Irish Sea
Berwick-upon-Tweed
Holy Island
R. Tweed
Cheviot Hills
Kielder Water
Tynemouth
Sunderland
Newcastle upon Tyne
Durham
Hartlepool
Middlesbrough
Teesside
Darlington
Whitby
Scarborough
North York Moors
Carlisle
Silloth
Solway Firth
Workington
Whitehaven
Cumbrian Mts
Helvellyn 949m
Scafell Pike 977m
Lake District
Ullswater
L. Windermere
Kendal
Snaefell 621m
Douglas
Ronaldsway
Barrow-in-Furness
Heysham
Morecambe Bay
Lancaster
Fleetwood
Blackpool
Preston
Southport
Pennines
R. Tyne
R. Wear
R. Tees
R. Lune
R. Ribble
R. Derwent
R. Mersey
R. Dee
R. Trent
Ouse
R. Humber
Leeds / Bradford
Bradford
Leeds
York
Burnley
Blackburn
Bolton
Huddersfield
Oldham
Knowsley
Liverpool
Manchester
Sheffield
Doncaster
Scunthorpe
Immingham
Kingston upon Hull
Humberside
Grimsby
Lincoln
Skegness
Boston
Chester
Crewe
Stoke-on-Trent
Stafford
Derby
Nottingham
Oswestry
A1
A69
A66
A65
A64
A63
A628
A46
A16
A17
A52
A523
A1(M)
M6
M55
M65
M66
M62
M61
M58
M53
M56
M63
M180
M1

Traffic congestion in and around large towns has increased year by year. Different solutions are being tried around the country. Bus lanes allow buses to travel faster than cars. This should attract more passengers on to the buses.

In Manchester a new tram-way has been laid. Large numbers of people can be taken quickly and cleanly through the city centre. Trams do not give off exhaust fumes, they run on electricity.

Attempts to attract more people to use the train depend on clean, comfortable, fast and reliable services.

rge thermal power stations have been built in the coal mining eas of Yorkshire and the east Midlands. Many jobs depend them. The pollution that they cause means that their future under threat.

Fact file England

Population	47 873 300
Highest mountain	Scafell Pike 977 m (3162 ft)
Longest river	Severn 354 km (220 miles)
Largest lake	Windermere 15 sq km (5.5 sq miles)

Interesting facts:

The River Severn has its source in Wales.

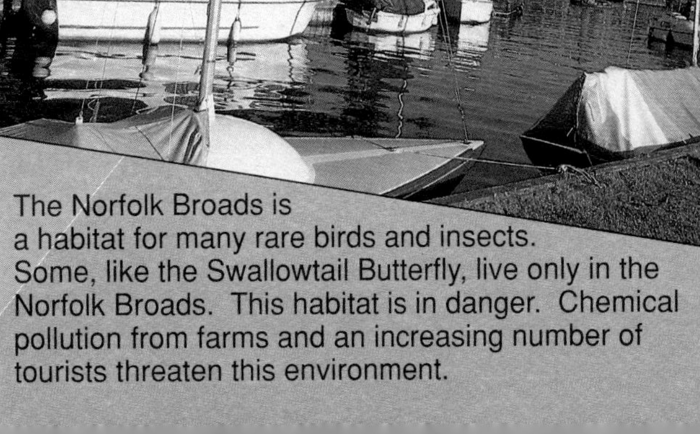

The Norfolk Broads is a habitat for many rare birds and insects. Some, like the Swallowtail Butterfly, live only in the Norfolk Broads. This habitat is in danger. Chemical pollution from farms and an increasing number of tourists threaten this environment.

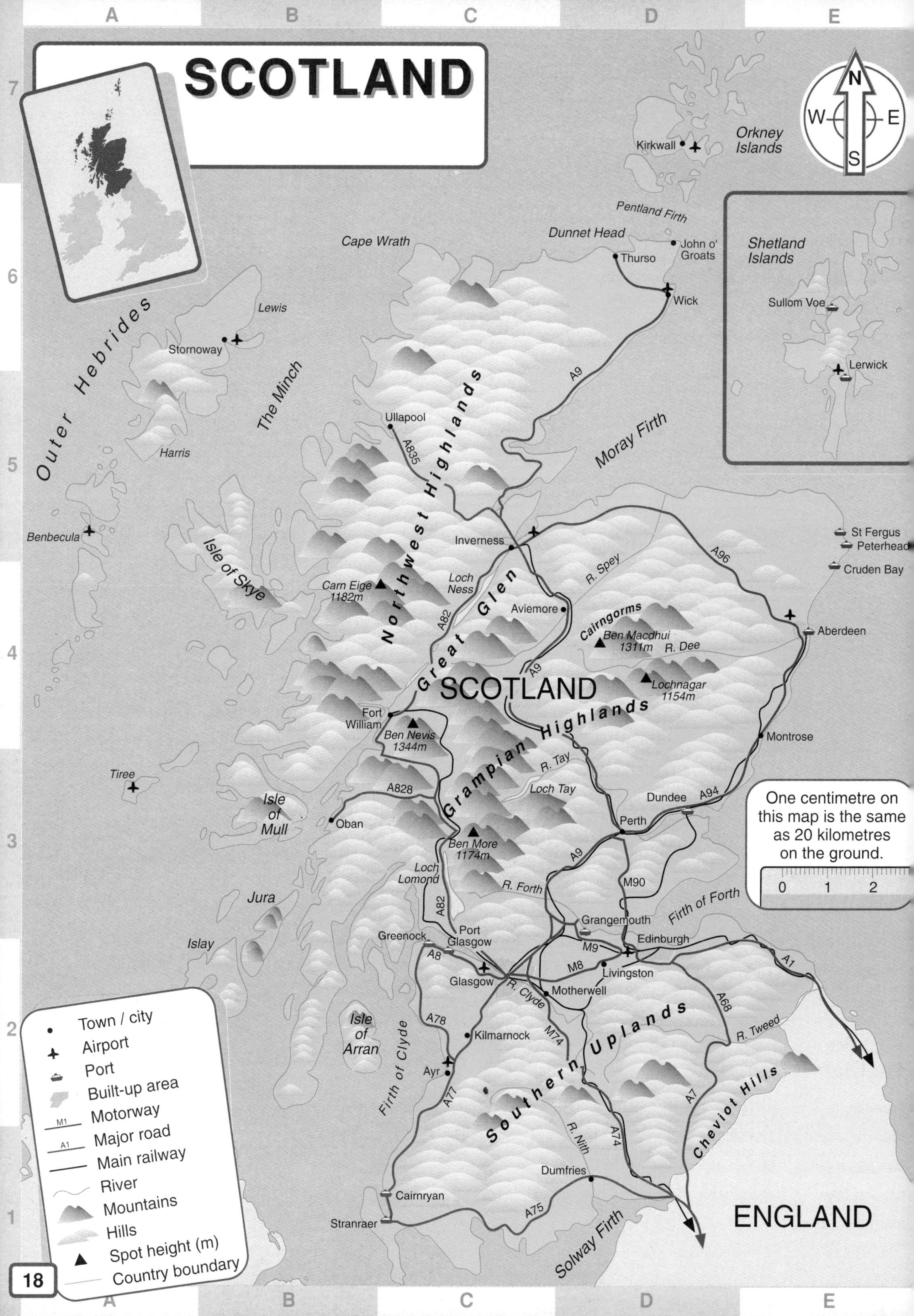
SCOTLAND
Orkney Islands
Kirkwall
Pentland Firth
Dunnet Head
John o' Groats
Thurso
Wick
Cape Wrath
Shetland Islands
Sullom Voe
Lerwick
Outer Hebrides
Lewis
Stornoway
The Minch
Harris
Ullapool
A835
A9
Moray Firth
Northwest Highlands
Benbecula
Isle of Skye
Inverness
Loch Ness
Carn Eige 1182m
Great Glen
A82
Aviemore
R. Spey
Cairngorms
Ben Macdhui 1311m
R. Dee
A96
St Fergus
Peterhead
Cruden Bay
Aberdeen
SCOTLAND
Lochnagar 1154m
Grampian Highlands
Fort William
Ben Nevis 1344m
Montrose
Tiree
Isle of Mull
A828
Oban
R. Tay
Loch Tay
Dundee
A94
Perth
Ben More 1174m
One centimetre on this map is the same as 20 kilometres on the ground.
0 1 2
Loch Lomond
R. Forth
M90
Jura
Islay
Firth of Forth
Grangemouth
Edinburgh
Greenock
Port Glasgow
A8
M9
M8
A1
Glasgow
Livingston
R. Clyde
Motherwell
A68
Isle of Arran
Firth of Clyde
A78
Kilmarnock
M74
Southern Uplands
R. Tweed
Ayr
A77
Cheviot Hills
A7
R. Nith
A74
Dumfries
Cairnryan
Stranraer
A75
Solway Firth
ENGLAND
Town / city
Airport
Port
Built-up area
Motorway
Major road
Main railway
River
Mountains
Hills
Spot height (m)
Country boundary
N
W
E
S
A B C D E
7 6 5 4 3 2 1

e on the cool, wet, western
ands has always been hard.
day many islands have been
serted. People have moved
the mainland to find jobs and
nore comfortable life. A way
life that has existed for
nerations is coming to an end.

Oil and gas were discovered beneath the North Sea in the 1970s. Today much of the oil is piped to Sullom Voe in the Shetlands and to Cruden Bay near Aberdeen. The main gas lines run to St Fergus north of Aberdeen. Many jobs have been created in the oil and gas industries.

Many people in Scotland are unhappy at being governed from London and want more control over what happens to their country. That could include deciding how oil and gas earnings should be spent.

Fact file Scotland

Population	5 102 400
Highest mountain	Ben Nevis 1 344 m (4 406 ft)
Longest river	Tay 188 km (117 miles)
Largest lake	Loch Lomond 70 sq km (27.5 sq miles)

Interesting facts:

The oldest rocks in the British Isles are in the West Highlands and Western Isles. They are almost 3 000 million years old.

Tourism is an important industry employing many thousands of people throughout Scotland. Glasgow, Scotland's largest city, is now a major tourist attraction. This has helped provide work for people who lost their jobs when older industries were run down.

Tourism needs to be managed. If too many tourists visit the wilder parts of Scotland, they could pose a threat to the wildlife which lives there. Golden eagles and wildcats were once common throughout Britain. It is vitally important that they continue to survive in the Scottish Highlands and that the tourist industry operates in harmony with the natural environment.

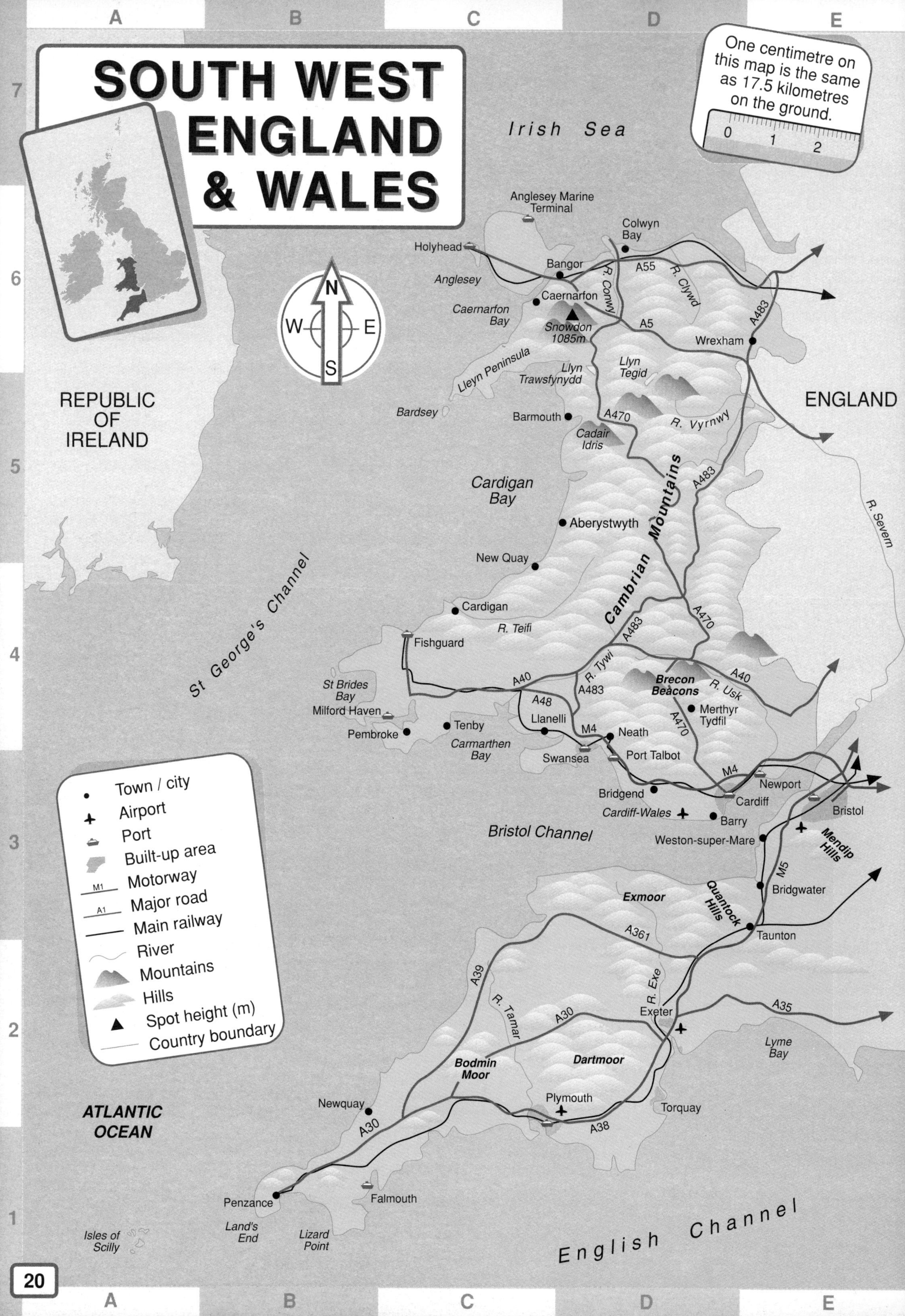
SOUTH WEST ENGLAND & WALES
One centimetre on this map is the same as 17.5 kilometres on the ground.
0 1 2
A B C D E
7 6 5 4 3 2 1
N W E S
Irish Sea
REPUBLIC OF IRELAND
ENGLAND
Anglesey Marine Terminal
Holyhead
Anglesey
Colwyn Bay
Bangor
A55
R. Clywd
R. Conwy
Caernarfon
Caernarfon Bay
Snowdon 1085m
A5
Wrexham
A483
Lleyn Peninsula
Llyn Trawsfynydd
Llyn Tegid
Bardsey
Barmouth
A470
R. Vyrnwy
Cadair Idris
Cardigan Bay
Cambrian Mountains
A483
R. Severn
Aberystwyth
New Quay
St George's Channel
Cardigan
R. Teifi
Fishguard
A483
A470
R. Tywi
A483
A40
St Brides Bay
Milford Haven
Pembroke
Tenby
Carmarthen Bay
A48
Llanelli
Brecon Beacons
R. Usk
A40
Merthyr Tydfil
A470
M4
Neath
Swansea
Port Talbot
M4
Newport
Bridgend
Cardiff
Cardiff-Wales
Barry
Bristol
Bristol Channel
Weston-super-Mare
Mendip Hills
M5
Bridgwater
Exmoor
Quantock Hills
Taunton
A361
A39
R. Exe
R. Tamar
A30
Exeter
A35
Lyme Bay
Bodmin Moor
Dartmoor
Plymouth
Torquay
Newquay
A30
A38
ATLANTIC OCEAN
Penzance
Falmouth
Land's End
Lizard Point
Isles of Scilly
English Channel
Town / city
Airport
Port
Built-up area
M1 Motorway
A1 Major road
Main railway
River
Mountains
Hills
Spot height (m)
Country boundary

There are no jobs here, so we are moving to London.

WALES | ENGLAND

We can afford a second home; we've decided to buy one in Wales.

For many years Welsh language and culture were in decline. Now attempts are being made to change this. Welsh-speaking schools are increasing and TV programmes in Welsh are more common. Welsh is once again a valued language. However young Welsh speaking people continue to leave Wales in order to find jobs. At the same time, English speakers buy homes in Wales for holidays or retirement. This demand for second homes drives up the prices of houses, making it even harder for young Welsh people to buy a home in the area where they were born.

Wales was once a major slate- and coal-producing country. Slate quarrying declined earlier this century, as more homes were built using tiles instead of slate. In the 1980s and 1990s many coal pits were closed. Thousands were thrown out of work. Efforts have been made to attract new industries to Wales.

Fact file Wales

Population	2 881 400
Highest mountain	Snowdon 1085 m (3561 ft)
Longest river	Usk 105 km (65 miles)
Largest lake	Llyn Tegid 4.5 sq km (1.5 sq miles)

Interesting facts:

Llyn Tegid is the largest *natural* lake. Larger lakes have been formed by dams.

Tourists from all over the world are attracted to Snowdonia. The castles along the coast are among the finest in Europe. The scenery of the mountains is breathtaking. Wild goats and rare plants can be seen on the higher, wilder slopes. Tourists are encouraged to respect this natural environment so that future generations will also enjoy it.

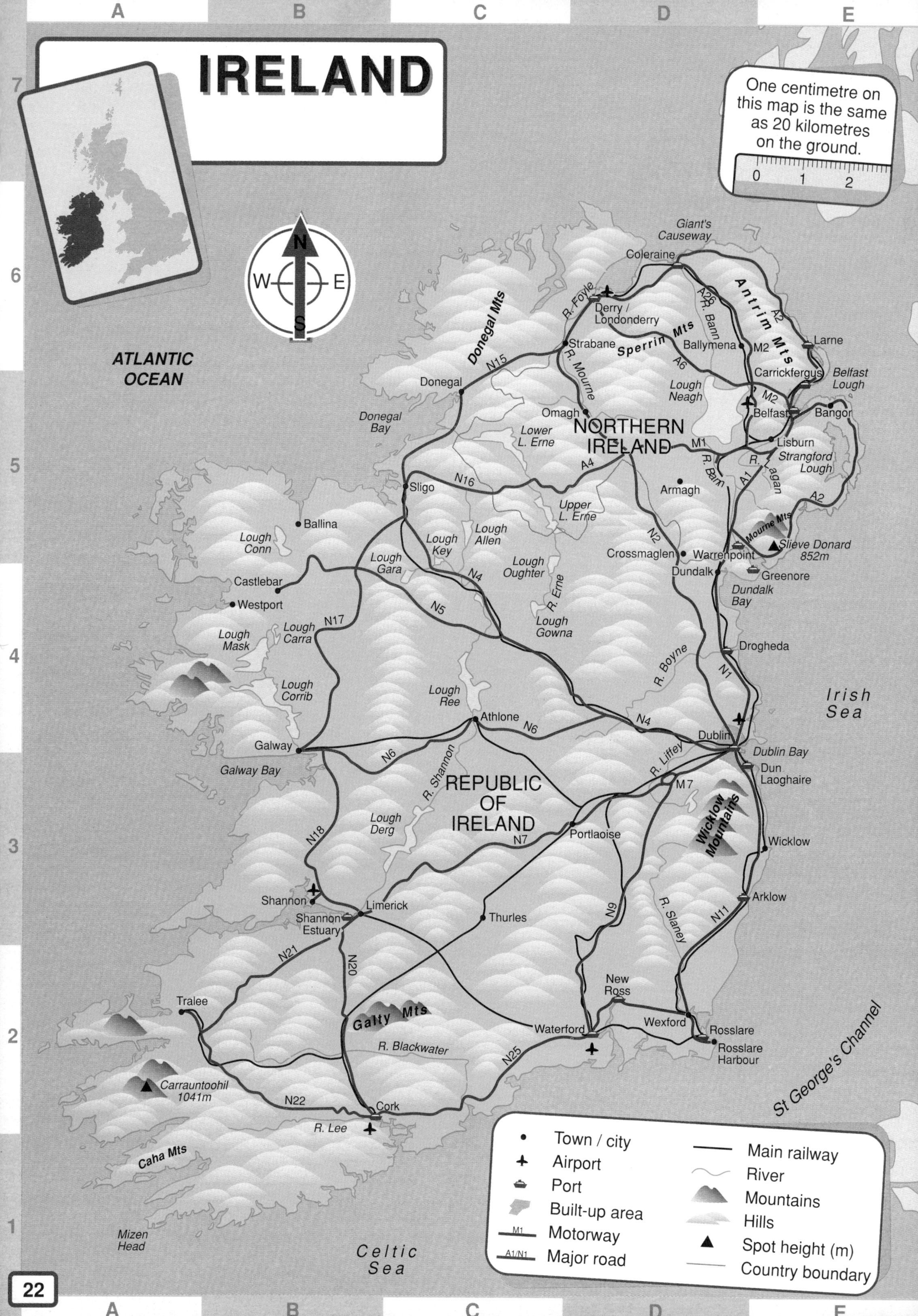
IRELAND
One centimetre on this map is the same as 20 kilometres on the ground.
0 1 2
A B C D E
7 6 5 4 3 2 1
ATLANTIC OCEAN
Irish Sea
Celtic Sea
St George's Channel
NORTHERN IRELAND
REPUBLIC OF IRELAND
Giant's Causeway
Coleraine
Antrim Mts
Derry / Londonderry
R. Foyle
Donegal Mts
Sperrin Mts
Strabane
Ballymena
Larne
Carrickfergus
Belfast Lough
Belfast
Bangor
Lough Neagh
Omagh
R. Mourne
Donegal
Donegal Bay
Lower L. Erne
Lisburn
Strangford Lough
Armagh
R. Bann
R. Lagan
Sligo
Ballina
Lough Conn
Upper L. Erne
Lough Allen
Lough Key
Lough Gara
Lough Oughter
Crossmaglen
Warrenpoint
Mourne Mts
Slieve Donard 852m
Greenore
Dundalk
Dundalk Bay
Castlebar
Westport
R. Erne
Lough Gowna
Lough Mask
Lough Carra
Lough Corrib
Drogheda
R. Boyne
Lough Ree
Athlone
Galway
Galway Bay
Dublin
Dublin Bay
Dun Laoghaire
R. Liffey
R. Shannon
Lough Derg
Portlaoise
Wicklow Mountains
Wicklow
Arklow
Shannon
Shannon Estuary
Limerick
Thurles
R. Slaney
New Ross
Wexford
Rosslare
Rosslare Harbour
Tralee
Galty Mts
R. Blackwater
Waterford
Carrauntoohil 1041m
Cork
R. Lee
Caha Mts
Mizen Head
N15 N16 A4 M1 A2 A26 A6 M2 A1 N2 N4 N5 N17 N6 N1 N18 N7 M7 N9 N11 N21 N20 N25 N22
Town / city
Airport
Port
Built-up area
Motorway
Major road
Main railway
River
Mountains
Hills
Spot height (m)
Country boundary
M1
A1/N1
N
W E
S

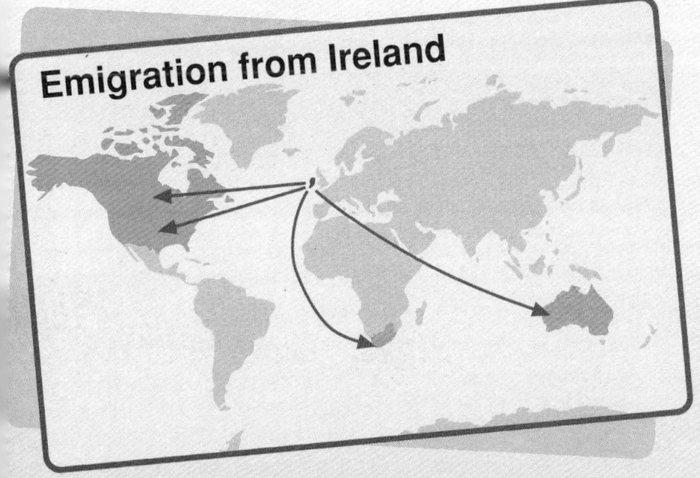
Emigration from Ireland

Irish communities are found throughout the English speaking world. In the USA, for example, they are proud to be known as 'Irish Americans'. Over the past 200 years Ireland has seen its people leave to start new lives in other places. This is still a serious issue in Ireland today. If young people leave they take skills, ambition and energy with them. Ways must be found to provide interesting, well paid jobs which will reduce emigration.

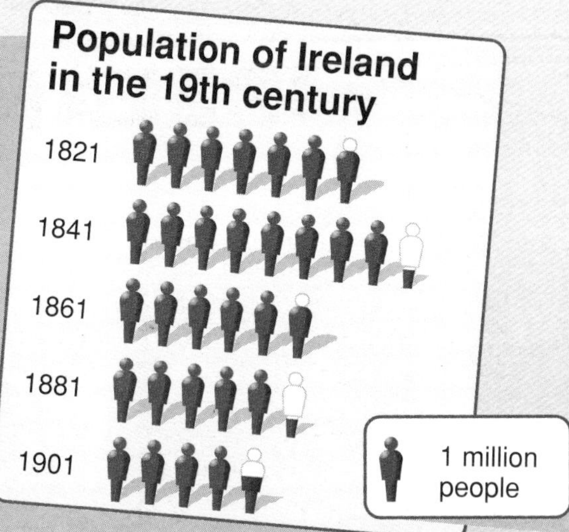
Population of Ireland in the 19th century
1821
1841
1861
1881
1901
1 million people

The potato blight of 1846 led to 1 million people dying and 1 million emigrating. By 1870 nearly 2 million Irish born people lived in the USA and threequarters of a million lived in Scotland, England and Wales.

Farming is a major industry in Ireland. The mild climate with its regular rainfall is ideal for the grass crops on which sheep and cattle feed.

The rivers and loughs of Ireland are famous. Anglers from all around the world are among the many tourists who visit Ireland every year.

I.R.A.
RADITIC

For many years the people of Belfast have lived with sectarian violence between extremist 'Loyalists' who want Ulster to remain part of the United Kingdom and extremist 'Republicans' who want British rule to end.

Fact file Ireland

Population	5 089 400
Highest mountain	Carrauntoohil 1 041 m (3 414 ft)
Longest river	Shannon 386 km (240 miles)
Largest lake	Lough Neagh 382 sq km (147 sq miles)

Interesting facts:

About 3.5 million people live in the Republic and 1.5 million live in Northern Ireland (Ulster).

British Isles index

A
Aberdeen Scotland **18 E4**
Aberystwyth Wales **20 D5**
Anglesey *Island* Wales **20 C6**
Anglesey Marine Terminal Wales **20 C6**
Antrim Mountains N. Ireland **22 E6**
Armagh N. Ireland **22 D5**
Ashford England **15 I3**
Aviemore Scotland **18 D4**
Avon *River* England **15 G4**
Ayr Scotland **18 C2**

B
Ballymena N. Ireland **22 D6**
Bangor N. Ireland **22 E5**
Bangor Wales **20 C6**
Bann *River* N. Ireland **22 D6**
Bardsey *Island* Wales **20 C5**
Barmouth Wales **20 D5**
Barrow-in-Furness England **16 B3**
Barry Wales **20 D3**
Basingstoke England **15 H3**
Belfast N. Ireland **22 E5**
Ben Macdhui *Mountain* Scotland **18 D4**
Ben Nevis *Mountain* Scotland **18 C4**
Benbecula *Island* Scotland **18 A5**
Berwick-upon-Tweed England **16 C6**
Bill of Portland *Feature* England **15 F2**
Birmingham England **15 G5**
Blackburn England **16 C3**
Blackpool England **16 B3**
Bodmin Moor *Feature* England **20 C2**
Bognor Regis England **15 H2**
Bolton England **16 C2**
Boston England **16 E1**
Bournemouth England **15 G2**
Bradford England **16 C3**
Brecon Beacons *Mountains* Wales **20 D4**
Bridgend Wales **20 D3**
Bridgwater England **20 E3**
Brighton England **15 I2**
Bristol England **15 F3**
Burnley England **16 C3**

C
Cadair Idris *Mountain* Wales **20 D5**
Caernarfon Wales **20 C6**
Cairngorms *Mountains* Scotland **18 D4**
Cairnryan Scotland **18 C1**
Cambrian Mountains Wales **20 D5**
Cambridge England **15 I5**
Canterbury England **15 J3**
Cape Wrath Scotland **18 C6**
Cardiff Wales **20 D3**
Cardigan Wales **20 C4**
Carlisle England **16 B4**
Carn Eige *Mountain* Scotland **18 B4**
Carmarthen Bay Wales **20 C4**
Carrickfergus N. Ireland **22 E5**
Celtic Sea UK/Rep. of Ireland **12 B2**
Channel Islands UK **15 F1**
Cheltenham England **15 F4**
Chester England **16 B2**
Cheviot Hills UK **12 C4**
Chiltern Hills England **15 H4**
Clyde *River* Scotland **18 C2**
Clywd *River* Wales **20 D6**
Colchester England **15 I4**
Coleraine N. Ireland **22 D6**
Colwyn Bay *Town* Wales **20 D6**
Conwy *River* Wales **20 D6**
Cork Rep. of Ireland **22 B2**
Cotswold Hills England **15 G4**
Coventry England **15 G5**
Cowes England **15 G2**
Crewe England **16 C2**
Crossmaglen N. Ireland **22 D5**
Cruden Bay *Town* Scotland **18 E4**
Cumbrian Mountains England **16 B4**

D
Darlington England **16 D4**
Dartmoor *Feature* England **20 D2**
Dee *River* Scotland **18 D4**
Derby England **16 D1**
Derry N. Ireland **22 D6**
Derwent *River* England **16 D3**
Doncaster England **16 D2**
Donegal Rep. of Ireland **22 C5**
Douglas UK **16 A3**
Dover England **15 J3**
Dublin Rep. of Ireland **22 D3**
Dumfries Scotland **18 D1**
Dundee Scotland **18 D3**
Dunnet Head *Cape* Scotland **18 D6**
Durham England **16 D4**

E
Edinburgh Scotland **18 D2**
ENGLAND UK **11**
Exe *River* England **20 D2**
Exeter England **20 D2**
Exmoor *Feature* England **20 D3**

F
Falmouth England **20 B1**
Felixstowe England **15 J4**
Fleetwood England **16 B3**
Folkestone England **15 J3**
Fort William Scotland **18 C4**
Forth *River* Scotland **18 C3**
Foyle *River* N. Ireland **22 D6**

G
Galway Rep. of Ireland **22 B4**
Giant's Causeway
Feature N. Ireland **22 D6**
Gillingham England **15 I3**
Glasgow Scotland **18 C2**
Gloucester England **15 F4**
Grampian Highlands Scotland **18 C3**
Grangemouth Scotland **18 D3**
Great Glen *Feature* Scotland **18 C4**
Great Ouse *River* England **15 I5**
Great Stour *River* England **15 J3**
Great Yarmouth England **15 J5**
Greenock Scotland **18 C2**
Grimsby England **16 E2**
Guernsey *Island* UK **15 F1**

H
Hartlepool England **16 D4**
Harwich England **15 J4**
Hastings England **15 I2**
Helvellyn *Mountain* England **16 B4**
Hereford England **15 F4**
Heysham England **16 B3**
Holy Island England **16 C6**
Holyhead Wales **20 C6**
Huddersfield England **16 C2**
Humber *Estuary* England **16 E2**

I
Immingham England **16 E2**
Inverness Scotland **18 C5**
Ipswich England **15 J4**
Isle of Arran *Island* Scotland **18 B2**
Isle of Man *Island* UK **16 A3**
Isle of Mull Scotland **18 B3**
Isle of Skye Scotland **18 B4**
Isle of Wight *Island* England **15 G2**
Isles of Scilly *Islands* UK **20 A1**

J
Jersey *Island* UK **15 F1**
John o'Groats Scotland **18 D6**
Jura *Island* Scotland **18 B3**

K
Kendal England **16 B3**
Kilmarnock Scotland **18 C2**
King's Lynn England **15 I5**
Kingston upon Hull England **16 E3**
Kirkwall Scotland **18 D7**

L
Lagan *River* N. Ireland **22 E5**
Lake District *Feature* England **16 B4**
Lake Windermere England **16 B4**
Lancaster England **16 C3**
Land's End *Cape* England **20 B1**
Larne N. Ireland **22 E6**
Leeds England **16 D3**
Leicester England **15 G5**
Lerwick Scotland **18 E6**
Lewis *Island* Scotland **18 B6**
Lichfield England **15 G5**
Liffey *River* Rep. of Ireland **22 D4**
Lincoln England **16 E2**
Lisburn N. Ireland **22 E4**
Littlehampton England **15 H2**
Liverpool England **16 B2**
Livingston Scotland **18 D2**
Lizard Point *Cape* England **20 B1**
Llanelli Wales **20 C4**
Lleyn Peninsula *Feature* Wales **20 C6**
Llyn Tegid *Lake* Wales **20 D5**
Llyn Trawsfynydd *Lake* Wales **20 D5**
Loch Lomond *Lake* Scotland **18 C3**
Loch Ness *Lake* Scotland **18 C4**
Loch Tay *Lake* Scotland **18 C3**
Lochnagar *Mountain* Scotland **18 D4**
London England **15 I4**
Londonderry N. Ireland **22 D6**
Lough Erne *Lake* N. Ireland **22 C5**
Lough Neagh *Lake* N. Ireland **22 D5**
Lowestoft England **15 J5**
Lune *River* England **16 C3**
Luton England **15 H4**

M
Manchester England **16 C2**
Margate England **15 J3**
Medway *River* England **15 I3**
Mendip Hills England **15 F3**
Mersey *River* England **16 C2**
Merthyr Tydfil Wales **20 D4**
Middlesbrough England **16 D4**
Milford Haven Wales **20 C4**
Milton Keynes England **15 H4**
Montrose Scotland **18 E4**
Motherwell Scotland **18 C2**
Mourne Mountains N. Ireland **22 E5**
Mourne *River* N. Ireland **22 D5**

N
Neath Wales **20 D4**
New Quay Wales **20 C4**
Newcastle upon Tyne England **16 D5**
Newhaven England **15 I2**
Newport Wales **20 E3**
Newquay England **20 B2**
Nith *River* Scotland **18 D1**
Norfolk Broads *Feature* England **15 J6**
North Downs *Feature* England **15 I3**
North York
Moors *Feature* England **16 D4**
Northampton England **15 H5**
NORTHERN IRELAND UK **22 D5**
Northwest Highlands Scotland **18 C5**
Norwich England **15 J5**
Nottingham England **16 D1**

O
Oban Scotland **18 B3**
Oldham England **16 C2**
Omagh N. Ireland **22 D5**
Orkney Islands Scotland **18 D7**
Oswestry England **16 B1**
Ouse *River* England **16 D3**
Outer Hebrides *Islands* Scotland **18 A5**
Oxford England **15 G4**

P
Pembroke Wales **20 C4**
Pennines *Mountains* England **16 C3**
Penzance England **20 B1**
Perth Scotland **18 D3**
Peterborough England **15 H5**
Peterhead Scotland **18 E5**
Plymouth England **20 C2**
Poole England **15 G2**
Port Glasgow Scotland **18 C3**
Port Talbot Wales **20 D4**
Portsmouth England **15 H2**
Preston England **16 B3**

Q
Quantock Hills England **20 D3**

R
Ramsgate England **15 J3**
Reading England **15 H3**
REPUBLIC OF IRELAND Europe **22**
Ribble *River* England **16 C3**
Rugby England **15 G5**
Rutland Water *Lake* England **15 H5**
Ryde England **15 G2**

S
Salisbury Plain *Feature* England **15**
Scafell Pike *Mountain* England **16**
Scarborough England **16 E4**
SCOTLAND UK **18**
Scunthorpe England **16 D2**
Severn *River* England **15 F5**
Shannon Rep. of Ireland **22 B3**
Shannon *River* Rep. of Ireland **22 C**
Sheerness England **15 I3**
Sheffield England **16 D2**
Shetland Islands Scotland **18 E6**
Shrewsbury England **15 F5**
Silloth England **16 B4**
Skegness England **16 E2**
Slaney *River* Rep. of Ireland **22 D3**
Slieve Donard *Mountain* N. Ireland **2**
Slough England **15 H4**
Snaefell *Mountain* UK **16 A3**
Snowdon *Mountain* Wales **20 D6**
Solent, The *Strait* England **15 G2**
South Downs *Feature* England **15 H**
Southampton England **15 G2**
Southend-on-Sea England **15 I4**
Southern Uplands
Mountains Scotland **18 D2**
Southport England **16 B2**
Sperrin Mountains N. Ireland **22 D6**
Spey *River* Scotland **18 D4**
St. Fergus Scotland **18 E5**
Stafford England **15 F6**
Stoke-on-Trent England **16 C1**
Stornoway Scotland **18 B6**
Stour *River* England **15 F2**
Strabane N. Ireland **22 D6**
Strangford Lough *Lake* N. Ireland **2**
Stranraer Scotland **18 C1**
Sullom Voe Scotland **18 E6**
Sunderland England **16 D4**
Swansea Wales **20 D3**
Swindon England **15 G4**

T
Tamar *River* England **20 C2**
Taunton England **20 E3**
Tay *River* Scotland **18 D3**
Tees *River* England **16 C4**
Teifi *River* Wales **20 C4**
Telford England **15 F5**
Tenby Wales **20 C4**
Test *River* England **15 G3**
Thames *River* England **15 G4**
Thurso Scotland **18 D6**
Tiree *Island* Scotland **18 A3**
Torquay England **20 D2**
Trent *River* England **16 D2**
Tweed *River* Scotland **18 E2**
Tyne *River* England **16 C4**
Tynemouth England **16 D5**
Tywi *River* Wales **20 D4**

U
Ullapool Scotland **18 C5**
Ullswater *Lake* England **16 B4**
Usk *River* Wales **20 D4**

V
Vyrnwy *River* Wales **20 D5**

W
WALES UK **20**
Walsall England **15 G5**
Warrenpoint N. Ireland **22 D5**
Warwick England **15 G4**
Waterford Rep. of Ireland **22 D2**
Watford England **15 H4**
Waveney *River* England **15 J5**
Weald, The *Feature* England **15 I2**
Wear *River* England **16 C4**
Weston-super-Mare England **20 E3**
Weymouth England **15 F2**
Whitby England **16 E4**
Whitehaven England **16 B4**
Wick Scotland **18 D6**
Wicklow Rep. of Ireland **22 E3**
Winchester England **15 G3**
Wolverhampton England **15 F5**
Worcester England **15 F5**
Workington England **16 B4**
Wrexham Wales **20 E6**

Y
York England **16 D3**

ANCIENT GREECE

Ancient Greece was not a single country as it is today. It was a large number of small independent states, each located around a city. The largest of these city states was Athens.

Each city state was proudly independent. A citizen of Athens was an Athenian first and a Greek second. People throughout Greece had much in common. They spoke the same language, used the same alphabet, worshipped the same gods and joined together for the Olympic Games.

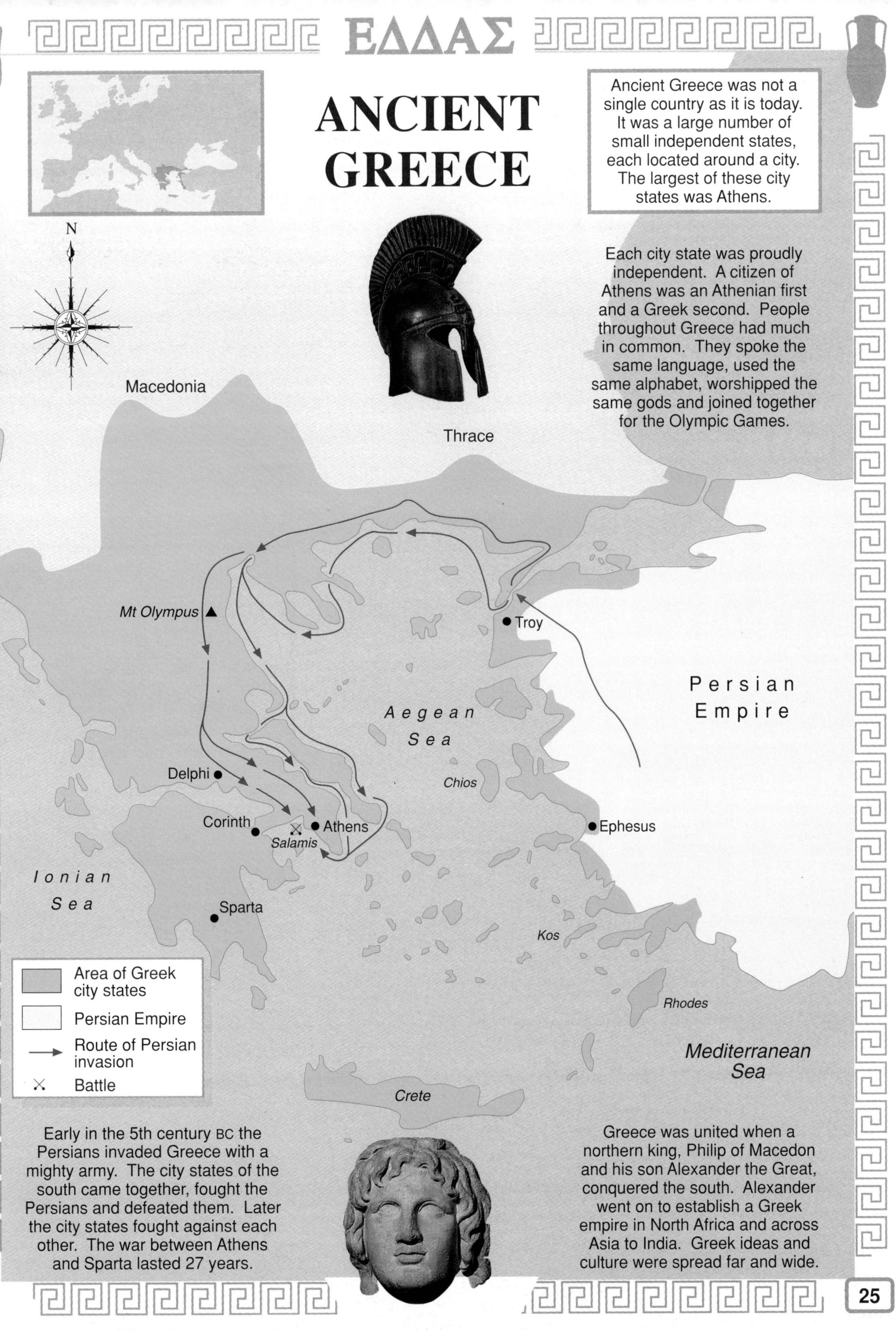
N
Macedonia
Thrace
Mt Olympus
Troy
Persian Empire
Aegean Sea
Chios
Delphi
Corinth
Athens
Salamis
Ephesus
Ionian Sea
Sparta
Kos
Rhodes
Mediterranean Sea
Crete
Area of Greek city states
Persian Empire
Route of Persian invasion
Battle

Early in the 5th century BC the Persians invaded Greece with a mighty army. The city states of the south came together, fought the Persians and defeated them. Later the city states fought against each other. The war between Athens and Sparta lasted 27 years.

Greece was united when a northern king, Philip of Macedon and his son Alexander the Great, conquered the south. Alexander went on to establish a Greek empire in North Africa and across Asia to India. Greek ideas and culture were spread far and wide.

INVADERS • AND • SETTLERS

The map shows the routes taken by invaders and settlers from their homelands to Britain. It covers the period from 55 BC when Julius Caesar landed in Britain, to the year AD 900 when the Viking invasions were almost at an end.

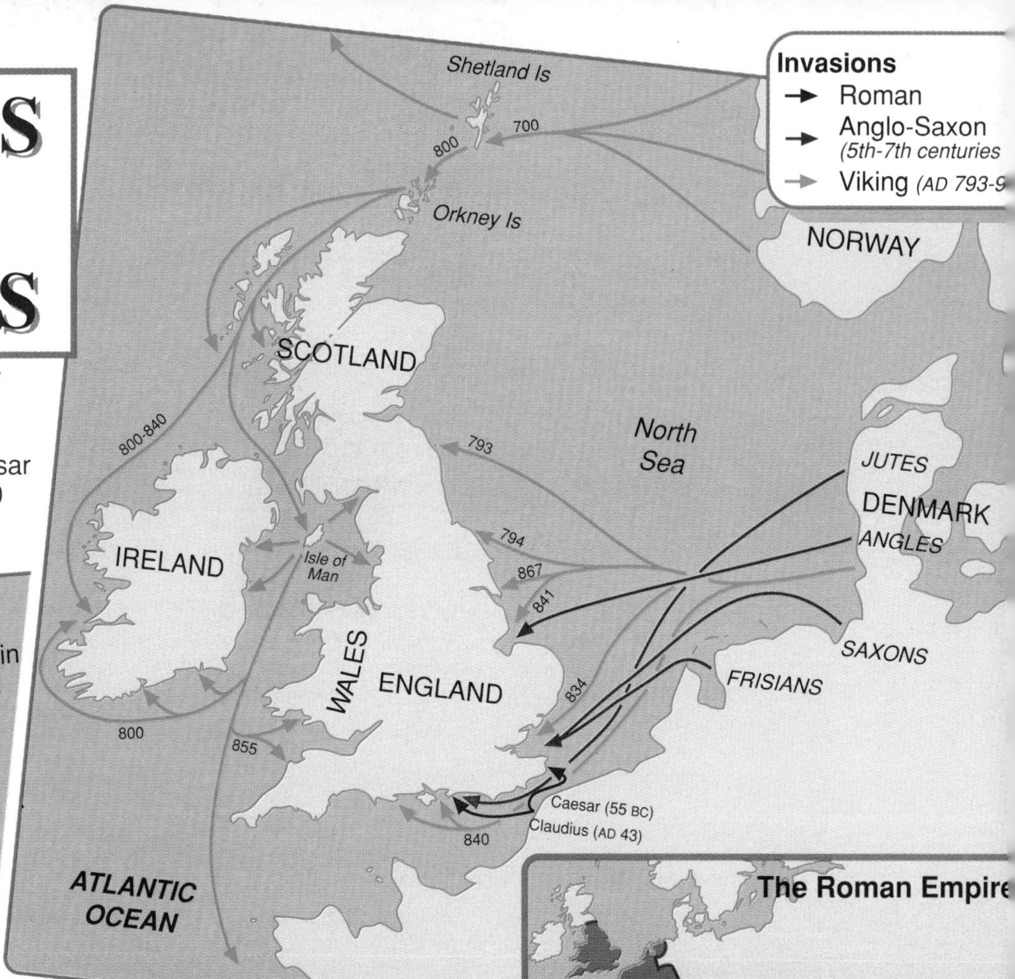

Invasions
Roman
Anglo-Saxon (5th-7th centuries
Viking (AD 793-9

Shetland Is
Orkney Is
NORWAY
SCOTLAND
North Sea
JUTES
DENMARK
ANGLES
SAXONS
FRISIANS
IRELAND
Isle of Man
WALES
ENGLAND
ATLANTIC OCEAN
Caesar (55 BC)
Claudius (AD 43)

Roman Britain

Although Julius Caesar visited Britain in 55 BC, the Romans did not stay. A full Roman invasion under Emperor Claudius took place in AD 43.

Scotland was always a problem for the Romans. They built Hadrian's Wall to keep the northern tribes out of their newly conquered land. Later they built a second wall, the Antonine Wall, but they never had complete control over Scotland.

Hadrian's Wall was 117 km long and 6.5 m high. It had a large fort every 8 km and a smaller one every 1.5 km.

Some Britons welcomed Roman rule. Others did not. The most important rebellion took place in AD 61 when the Iceni tribe, led by Boudicca, fought and almost defeated the Roman army.

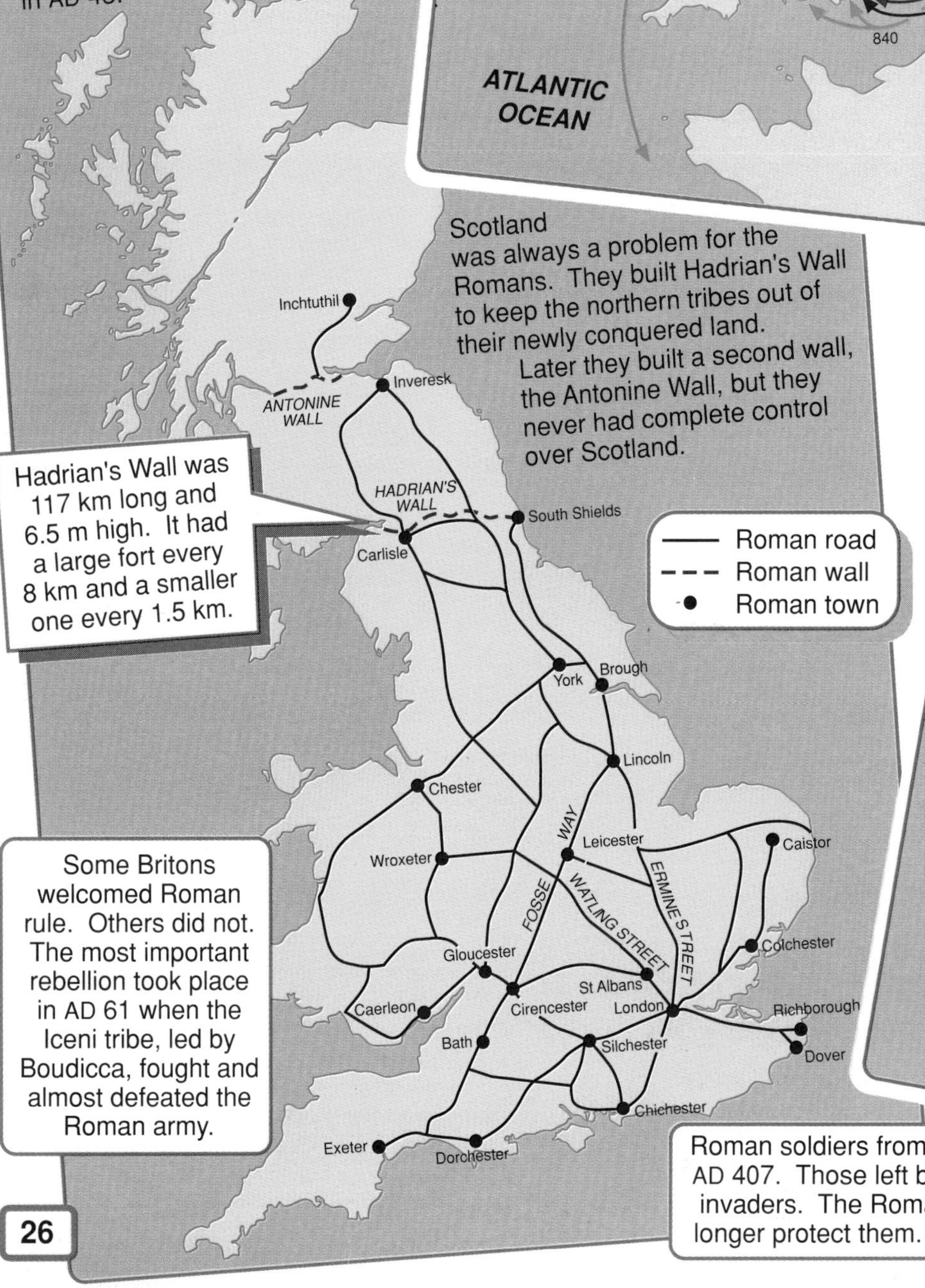

Roman road
Roman wall
Roman town

Inchtuthil
Inveresk
ANTONINE WALL
HADRIAN'S WALL
South Shields
Carlisle
York
Brough
Lincoln
Chester
Leicester
FOSSE WAY
WATLING STREET
ERMINE STREET
Caistor
Wroxeter
Gloucester
Colchester
St Albans
Caerleon
Cirencester
London
Richborough
Bath
Silchester
Dover
Chichester
Exeter
Dorchester

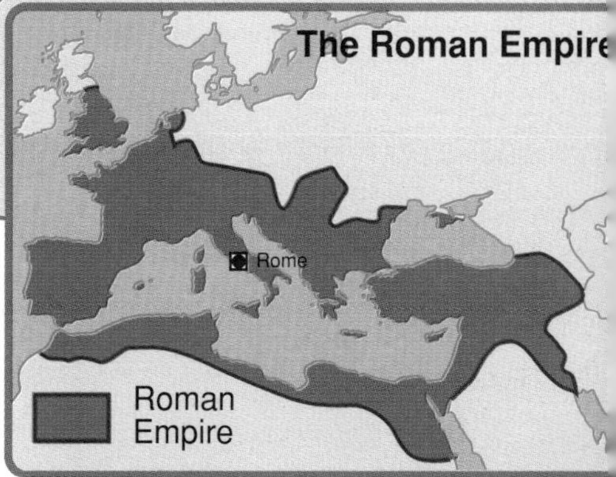

The Roman Empire

Rome
Roman Empire

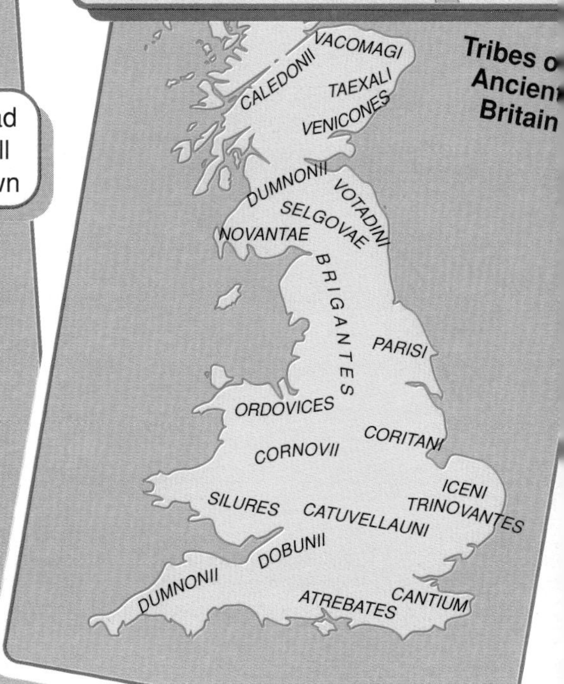

Tribes of Ancient Britain

VACOMAGI
CALEDONII
TAEXALI
VENICONES
DUMNONII
VOTADINI
SELGOVAE
NOVANTAE
BRIGANTES
PARISI
ORDOVICES
CORITANI
CORNOVII
ICENI
TRINOVANTES
SILURES
CATUVELLAUNI
DOBUNII
DUMNONII
ATREBATES
CANTIUM

Roman soldiers from Britain went to fight in continental Europe in AD 407. Those left behind could not defend Britain from the new invaders. The Roman Emperor told the British that he could no longer protect them. From AD 409 the British were on their own.

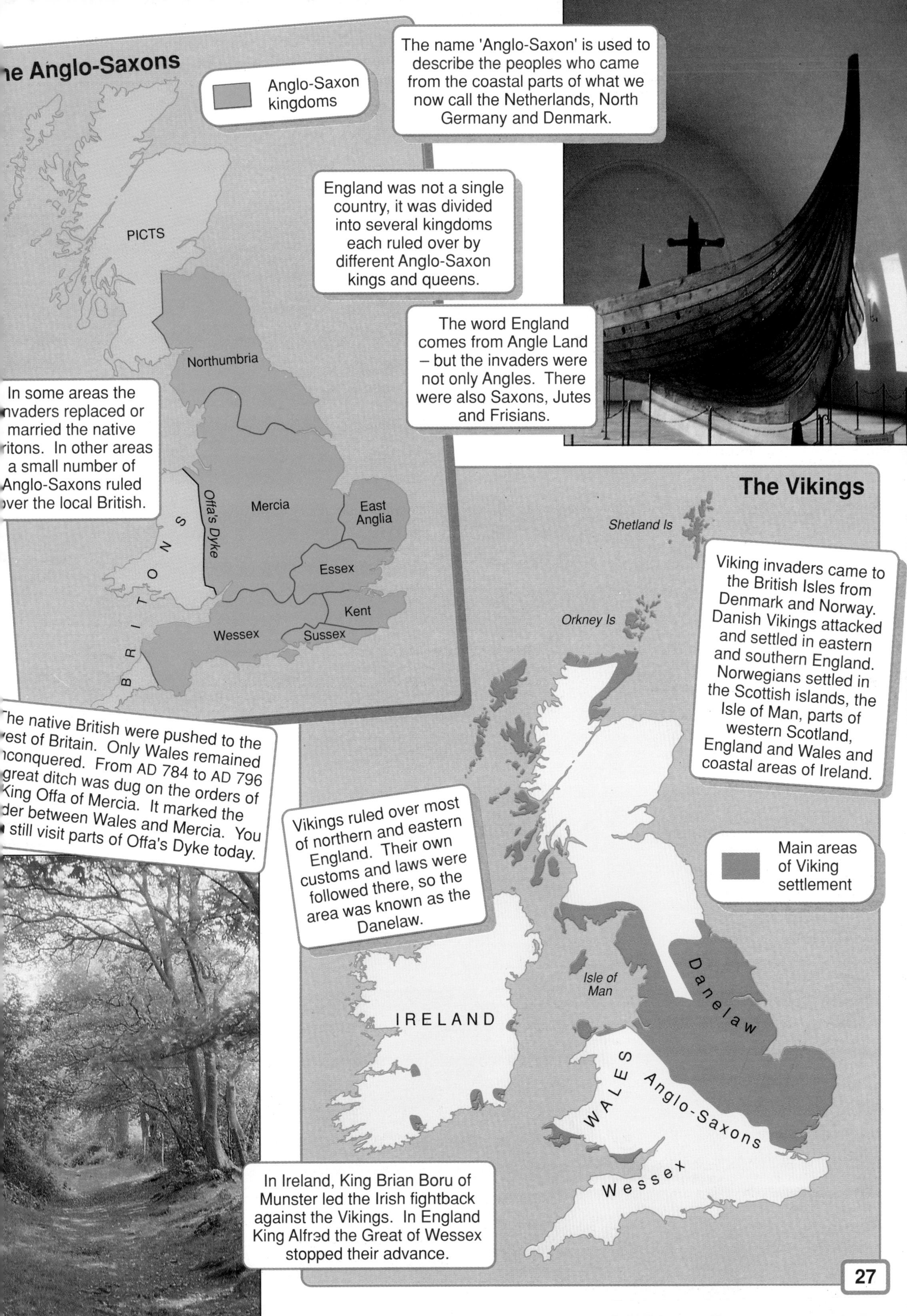

he Anglo-Saxons
Anglo-Saxon kingdoms
The name 'Anglo-Saxon' is used to describe the peoples who came from the coastal parts of what we now call the Netherlands, North Germany and Denmark.
England was not a single country, it was divided into several kingdoms each ruled over by different Anglo-Saxon kings and queens.
The word England comes from Angle Land – but the invaders were not only Angles. There were also Saxons, Jutes and Frisians.
PICTS
Northumbria
Mercia
East Anglia
Essex
Kent
Wessex
Sussex
Offa's Dyke
BRITONS
In some areas the nvaders replaced or married the native ritons. In other areas a small number of Anglo-Saxons ruled ver the local British.
he native British were pushed to the est of Britain. Only Wales remained nconquered. From AD 784 to AD 796 great ditch was dug on the orders of King Offa of Mercia. It marked the der between Wales and Mercia. You still visit parts of Offa's Dyke today.
The Vikings
Shetland Is
Orkney Is
Viking invaders came to the British Isles from Denmark and Norway. Danish Vikings attacked and settled in eastern and southern England. Norwegians settled in the Scottish islands, the Isle of Man, parts of western Scotland, England and Wales and coastal areas of Ireland.
Vikings ruled over most of northern and eastern England. Their own customs and laws were followed there, so the area was known as the Danelaw.
Main areas of Viking settlement
Isle of Man
IRELAND
Danelaw
WALES
Anglo-Saxons
Wessex
In Ireland, King Brian Boru of Munster led the Irish fightback against the Vikings. In England King Alfred the Great of Wessex stopped their advance.

TUDOR AND STUART TIMES
The Armada

In 16th century Europe, there were many conflicts between Catholics and Protestants. Elizabeth I of England was a Protestant. She became Queen on the death of her half sister Queen Mary. Mary was a Catholic and married to King Philip II of Spain. Philip was angry with Elizabeth. He believed she was treating Catholics badly in England and that she was helping Protestants in the Netherlands which was a part of his Empire.

(1) Philip had a large army in the Netherlands. He sent a great fleet of ships (Armada) from Spain. The plan was to meet the army and carry it across the English Channel, ready for an attack on London.

(2) As the Spanish sailed through the Channel they fought the English navy. The Armada had to wait at Calais because the Spanish army was not ready. The English fleet attacked. The next day a great battle took place at Gravelines. Many Spanish ships were damaged.

(3) The Spanish decided not to risk another battle in the Channel but to try to reach home by sailing around Scotland and Ireland.

(4) Storms drove many Spanish ships on to the shores of Ireland. Survivors were killed as they came ashore because the English feared the Spanish Catholic sailors might join the Irish Catholic people and fight against the English.
When the remaining Spanish ships reached home, so many men had died and the fleet was so badly damaged that the invasion of England was no longer possible.

N
15 Aug 1588
SCOTLAND
North Sea
IRELAND
WALES
ENGLAND
London
8 Aug 1588
Gravelines
Calais
SPANISH NETHERLANDS
Spanish Army
19 July 1588
English Channel
ATLANTIC OCEAN
La Coruña
Santander
Sept - Oct 1588
70 ships
PORTUGAL
Madrid
SPAIN
Lisbon
May 1588
150 ships
Cadiz

Area under English control
Area under Spanish control
Route of Spanish Armada
Spanish ships
English ships
Area of fighting
Battle
Storm

EXPLORATION AND ENCOUNTERS 1450 to 1550

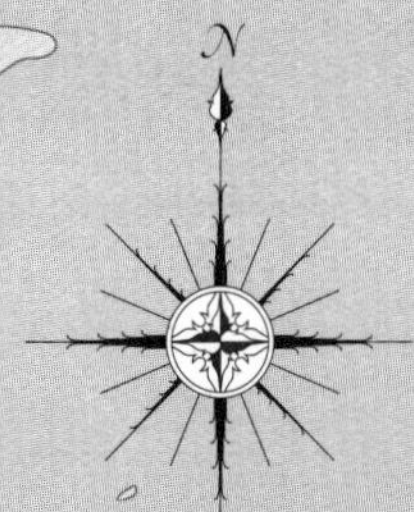
N

Arctic Circle

In the 15th century most educated people knew that the earth was round. Explorers believed they could find a short route to Asia by sailing west. What they did not know was that the continents of North and South America were in the way.

John Cabot searched for a northern route to Asia. He reached Newfoundland.

John Cabot (1497)

ENGLAND

Bristol

Newfoundland

FRANCE

EUROPE

NORTH AMERICA

NORTH ATLANTIC OCEAN

PORTUGAL

SPAIN

Lisbon

Cadiz

Christopher Columbus (1492)

San Salvador I

Tropic of Cancer

Hernando Cortez

Area of Aztec civilization

NORTH PACIFIC OCEAN

Christopher Columbus reached the Caribbean Islands in 1492. He crossed the Atlantic three more times and explored the mainland, however he always believed he was in Asia.

AFRICA

Equator

The explorers were soon followed by conquering armies. Hernando Cortez conquered the Aztec Empire (modern Mexico). Francisco Pizarro conquered the Inca Empire (modern Peru). The lives of the people of the Americas were changed forever.

Francisco Pizarro

SOUTH AMERICA

Ferdinand Magellan (1520)

Area of Inca civilization

Tropic of Capricorn

SOUTH PACIFIC OCEAN

Ferdinand Magellan sailed south hoping to find a sea route through South America. Eventually he discovered a 600km passage at the tip of the continent. He sailed through it and reached the Pacific Ocean.

SOUTH ATLANTIC OCEAN

Magellan's Strait

Explorers' Routes

- Columbus
- Cabot
- Magellan

Conquerors' Routes

- Cortez
- Pizarro

Empires of the Americas

- Aztecs
- Incas

VICTORIAN BRITAIN

1837

1901

Victoria became Queen in 1837. She died in 1901. Great changes took place in Britain during her reign.

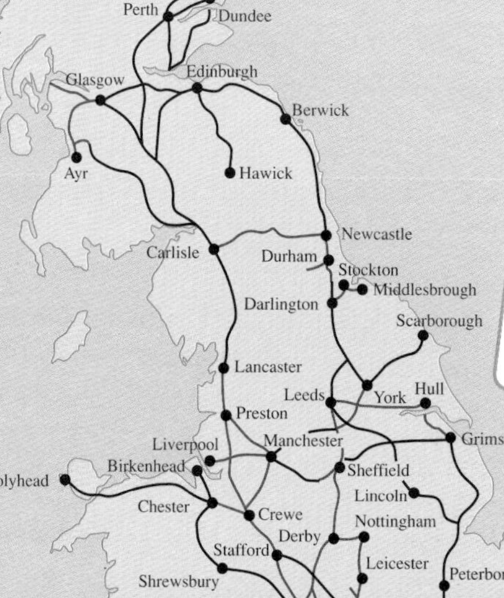
Railways
Built before 1841
Built by 1850
Aberdeen
Montrose
Arbroath
Perth
Dundee
Glasgow
Edinburgh
Berwick
Ayr
Hawick
Newcastle
Carlisle
Durham
Stockton
Middlesbrough
Darlington
Scarborough
Lancaster
Leeds
York
Hull
Preston
Liverpool
Manchester
Grimsby
Birkenhead
Holyhead
Sheffield
Lincoln
Chester
Crewe
Nottingham
Derby
Stafford
Leicester
Peterborough
Yarmouth
Norwich
Shrewsbury
Birmingham
Rugby
Ely
Cambridge
Gloucester
Colchester
Swansea
Oxford
Whitstable
Cardiff
London
Canterbury
Bristol
Guildford
Dover
Salisbury
Gosport
Lewes
Southampton
St Leonards
Exeter
Dorchester
Portsmouth
Brighton
Newhaven
Plymouth

In the early part of the 19th century most goo travelled by canal. This was slow a affected by ice in winter and water sho in summer. The railways changed all The world's first public steam railway between Stockton and Darlington in 1

The first inter-city railw ran between Liverpoo and Manchester in 183 The map shows the gre increase in railways up to 1850.

The population of London rose from 2 685 000 in 1851 to 6 586 000 in 1901. It was the largest city in the world.

City population

1851 1901

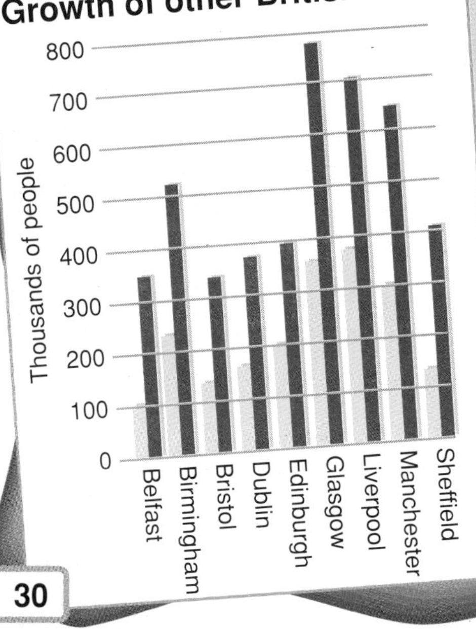
Growth of other British cities
Thousands of people
800
700
600
500
400
300
200
100
0
Belfast
Birmingham
Bristol
Dublin
Edinburgh
Glasgow
Liverpool
Manchester
Sheffield

Railways made trade quicker and cheaper. British cities grew rapidly as people moved there to work in factories and mills. The chart shows the population of Britain's main cities in 1851 and 1901.

The railways and factories needed coa for fuel. Coal producti in Victorian Britain increased enormousl

Coal production

1840
34 200 tons

1901
222 562 tons

THE BRITISH EMPIRE

Britain, like other European countries, began to establish an empire in the 16th and 17th centuries. Some parts of the Empire rebelled against rule from London. The USA fought and declared its independence in 1776.

The growth of empire continued into the 19th century. In 1901 the British Empire covered one quarter of the world's surface. One in four of the world's population was ruled over by Queen Victoria.

CANADA
UNITED KINGDOM
GIBRALTAR
MALTA
CYPRUS
BALUCHISTAN
UPPER BURMA
BERMUDA
BAHAMAS
BRITISH HONDURAS
JAMAICA
Leeward Is
BARBADOS
TRINIDAD
BRITISH GUIANA
EGYPT
INDIA
BURMA
NIGERIA
ANGLO EGYPTIAN SUDAN
GAMBIA
SIERRA LEONE
GOLD COAST
BUGANDA
BRITISH SOMALILAND
MALAYA
BORNEO
NORTH RHODESIA
BRITISH EAST AFRICA
Ascension
SOUTH RHODESIA
NYASALAND
St Helena
BECHUANALAND
PAPUA NEW GUINEA
FIJI
AUSTRALIA
NATAL
TRANSVAAL
CAPE PROVINCE
ORANGE FREE STATE
The British Empire at the end of Queen Victoria's reign
NEW ZEALAND
Falkland Is
Georgia

Most of the population of countries like Canada, Australia and New Zealand were descended from British settlers. These countries made many of their own decisions.

Some countries, like India, had been part of the Empire for a long time. Most of the soldiers and officials in British India were Indians.

In Africa much of the Empire was 'new', brought under British control in the second half of Queen Victoria's reign.

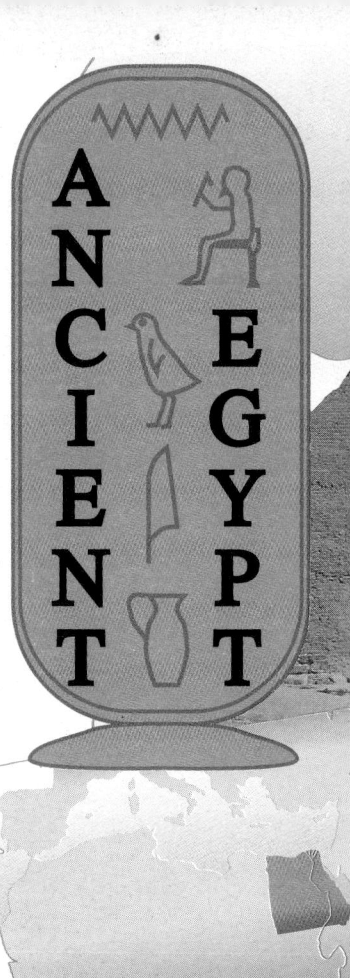

ANCIENT
EGYPT

Mediterranean Sea
Nile Delta
Alexandria
LOWER EGYPT

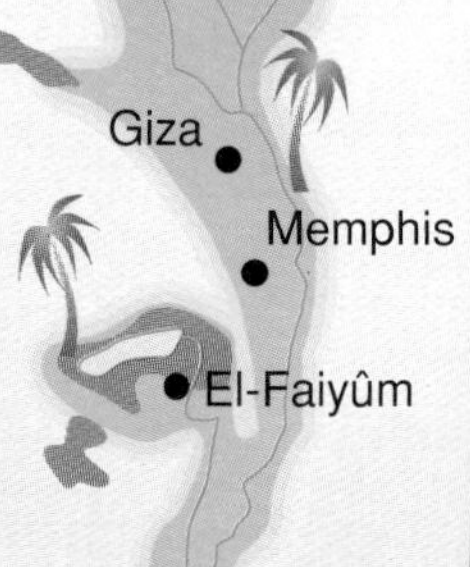

Giza
Memphis
El-Faiyûm
Bhar Yusaf

Pyramid and sphinx at Giza

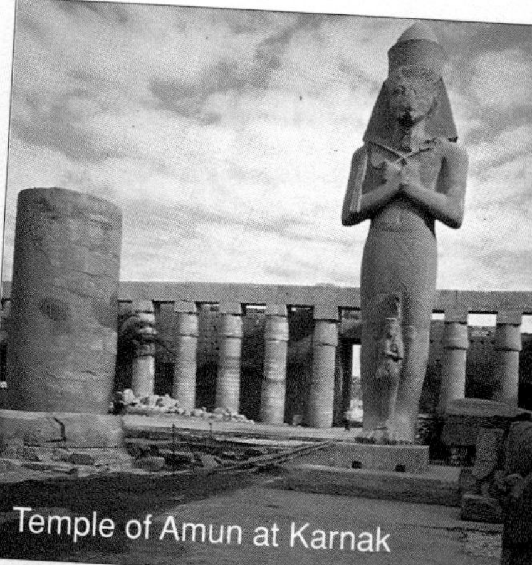

Temple of Amun at Karnak

Nile
Eastern Desert
Red Sea
UPPER EGYPT

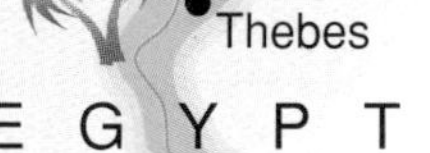

Karnak
Thebes
N
Aswan
Abu Simbel

The Inundation

August and September
(flooding)

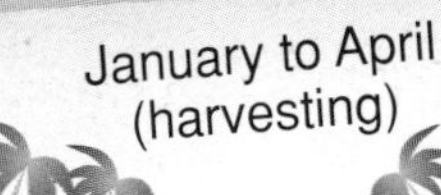

January to April
(harvesting)

The Nile was at its lowest level in June. It rose in July and flooded in August and September. In October and November, as the water level fell, the crops were sown. The main crops were cereals for bread, barley for beer, vegetables, fruit especially dates and sesame for oil. These were harvested from January to April before the next flood.

Abu Simbel, Temple of Rameses II

River
Fertile strip
Land below sea level

WHOSE OCEAN?

The sea covers more than 70% of the Earth. The largest ocean is the Pacific which is four times bigger than Asia. The seas are rich in life but today that life is under threat.

'he Mediterranean Sea is adly polluted. Most of the ollution comes from the and. Chemicals used in arming, industrial waste and ewage all pour into the sea.

Six million tonnes of oil enter the Earth's oceans every year. Some of this is accidental but much is caused by oil tankers 'washing-out' their tanks.

pecies at risk

Vhale numbers have been greatly educed by hunting. Campaigns rom conservationists have reduced, ut not stopped, whaling. Other pecies such as haddock, herring and nackerel have also been overfished.

.arge factory ships from Japan and Europe travel jreat distances to fish in the seas off West Africa. 'hese ships can handle up to 1 000 tonnes of fish a day. Most of this fish will be used as fertiliser on farms.

.ocal fishing people can only watch as their traditional catch is taken ar away.

Fishing with narrow-mesh nets in the Indian and Pacific Oceans has killed many dolphins and porpoises. Today these nets are made of material which does not rot. Even nets which have broken away from ships continue to trap and kill sea life. When your family buys tins of tuna, check that the tin tells you that care was taken not to catch mammals like dolphins. If not, what can you do?

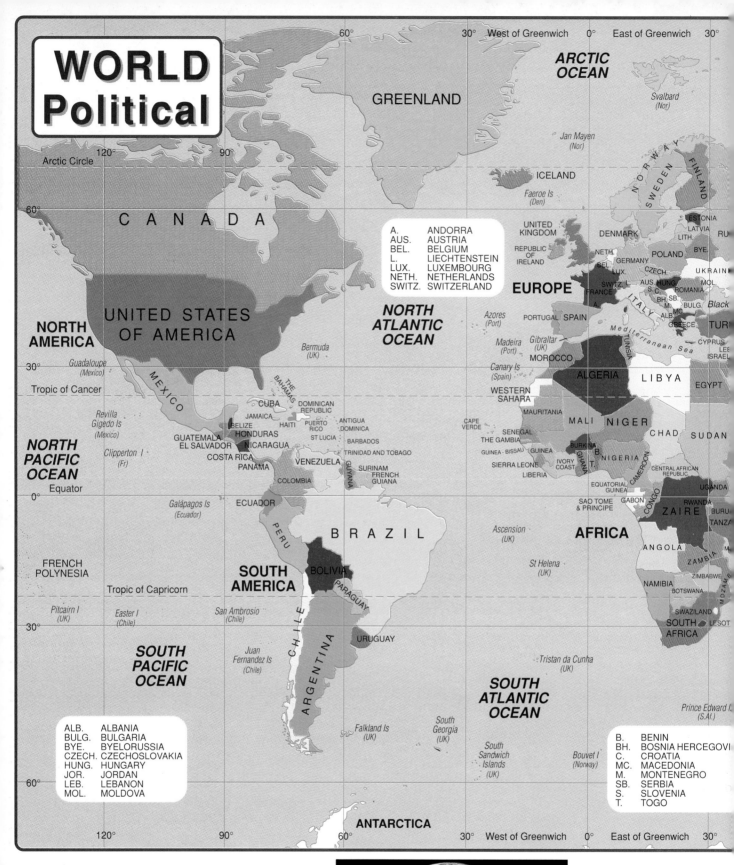

WORLD Political

60° 30° West of Greenwich 0° East of Greenwich 30°

ARCTIC OCEAN

GREENLAND

Svalbard (Nor)

Jan Mayen (Nor)

120° 90°

Arctic Circle

ICELAND

Faeroe Is (Den)

NORWAY SWEDEN FINLAND

60°

CANADA

A.	ANDORRA
AUS.	AUSTRIA
BEL.	BELGIUM
L.	LIECHTENSTEIN
LUX.	LUXEMBOURG
NETH.	NETHERLANDS
SWITZ.	SWITZERLAND

UNITED KINGDOM
REPUBLIC OF IRELAND
DENMARK
ESTONIA
LATVIA
LITH.
RU
NETH.
GERMANY
POLAND
BYE.
BEL.
LUX.
CZECH.
UKRAIN
AUS. HUNG.
MOL.
SWITZ. L.
S. C.
ROMANIA
FRANCE
BH. SB.
M.
BULG.
Black
EUROPE
A.
ITALY
MC.
ALB.
GREECE
TUR

NORTH ATLANTIC OCEAN

UNITED STATES OF AMERICA

NORTH AMERICA

Azores (Port)
PORTUGAL
SPAIN
Madeira (Port)
Gibraltar (UK)
Mediterranean Sea
CYPRUS
LEB
ISRAEL
TUNISIA
Bermuda (UK)
MOROCCO

30°
Guadaloupe (Mexico)
Tropic of Cancer
MEXICO
THE BAHAMAS
Canary Is (Spain)
ALGERIA
LIBYA
EGYPT
WESTERN SAHARA
CUBA
DOMINICAN REPUBLIC
Revilla Gigedo Is (Mexico)
JAMAICA
HAITI
PUERTO RICO
ANTIGUA
DOMINICA
BELIZE
HONDURAS
GUATEMALA
EL SALVADOR
NICARAGUA
ST LUCIA
BARBADOS
TRINIDAD AND TOBAGO
COSTA RICA
PANAMA
VENEZUELA
GUYANA
SURINAM
FRENCH GUIANA
COLOMBIA
MAURITANIA
MALI
NIGER
CHAD
SUDAN
CAPE VERDE
SENEGAL
THE GAMBIA
GUINEA - BISSAU
GUINEA
BURKINA
B.
GHANA
T.
NIGERIA
SIERRA LEONE
IVORY COAST
LIBERIA
CAMEROON
CENTRAL AFRICAN REPUBLIC
EQUATORIAL GUINEA
UGANDA

NORTH PACIFIC OCEAN

Clipperton I (Fr)

Equator
0°
Galápagos Is (Ecuador)
ECUADOR
SAO TOME & PRINCIPE
GABON
CONGO
RWANDA
ZAIRE
BURU
TANZ
PERU
BRAZIL
Ascension (UK)
AFRICA
ANGOLA
M
ZAMBIA
FRENCH POLYNESIA
BOLIVIA
SOUTH AMERICA
St Helena (UK)
ZIMBABWE
NAMIBIA
BOTSWANA
MOZAMB
Tropic of Capricorn
PARAGUAY
Pitcairn I (UK)
Easter I (Chile)
San Ambrosio (Chile)
CHILE
SWAZILAND
SOUTH AFRICA
LESOT
30°
URUGUAY
ARGENTINA
Juan Fernandez Is (Chile)
Tristan da Cunha (UK)

SOUTH PACIFIC OCEAN

SOUTH ATLANTIC OCEAN

Prince Edward I. (S.Af.)

ALB.	ALBANIA
BULG.	BULGARIA
BYE.	BYELORUSSIA
CZECH.	CZECHOSLOVAKIA
HUNG.	HUNGARY
JOR.	JORDAN
LEB.	LEBANON
MOL.	MOLDOVA

Falkland Is (UK)
South Georgia (UK)
South Sandwich Islands (UK)
Bouvet I (Norway)

B.	BENIN
BH.	BOSNIA HERCEGOVI
C.	CROATIA
MC.	MACEDONIA
M.	MONTENEGRO
SB.	SERBIA
S.	SLOVENIA
T.	TOGO

60°

ANTARCTICA

120° 90° 60° 30° West of Greenwich 0° East of Greenwich 30°

The Earth is a sphere. Satellite photographs give us a clear picture of the Earth in space. A globe provides a good model of the Earth, however it is not easy to carry a globe around or keep it in a bag! To provide information in an easy-to-read way the Earth needs to be shown on a flat map. The problem with turning a sphere into a map is that parts of the sphere need to be stretched to fit the paper.

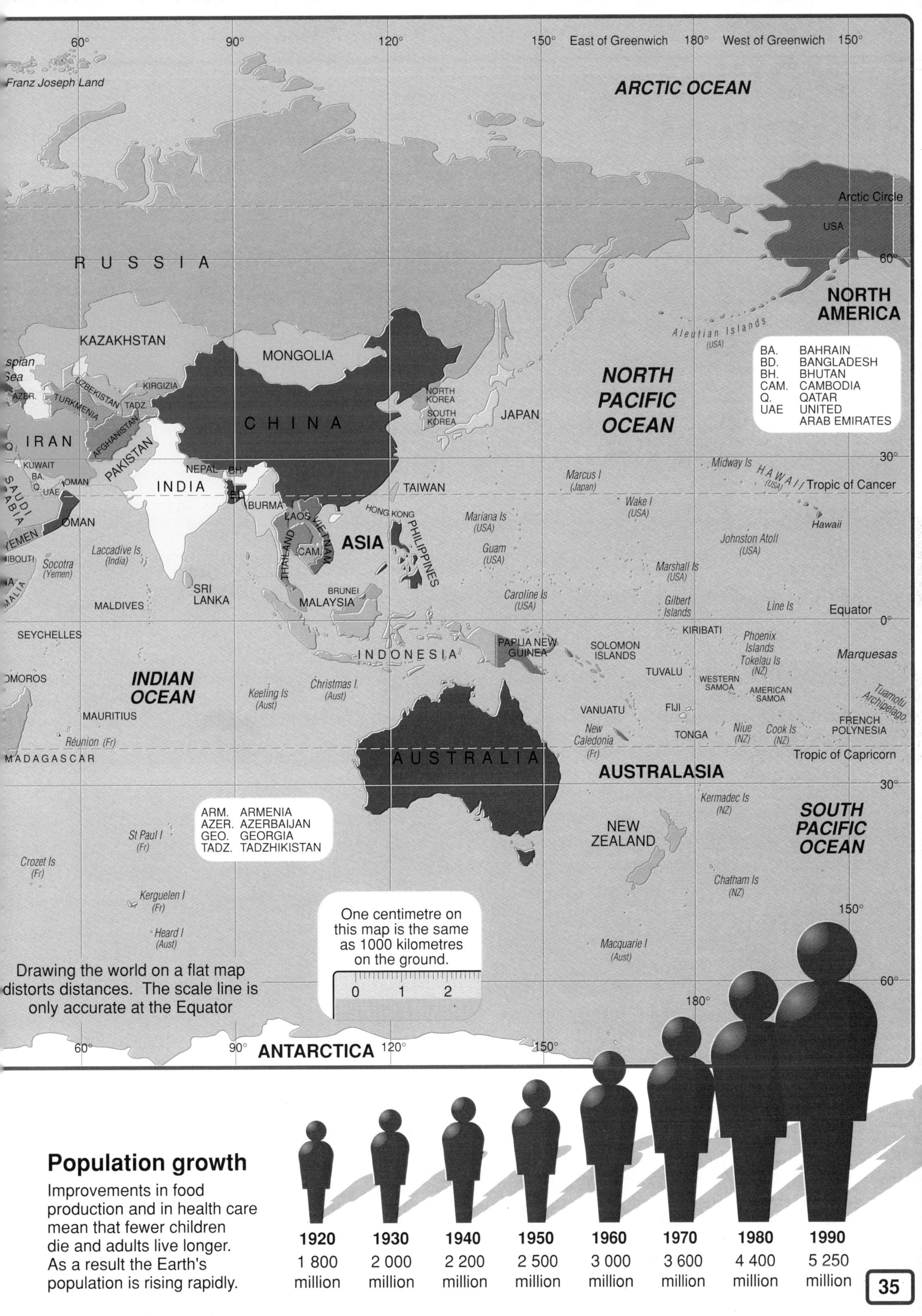

60° 90° 120° 150° East of Greenwich 180° West of Greenwich 150°
Franz Joseph Land
ARCTIC OCEAN
Arctic Circle
USA
60°
R U S S I A
NORTH AMERICA
KAZAKHSTAN
MONGOLIA
Aleutian Islands (USA)
BA. BAHRAIN
BD. BANGLADESH
BH. BHUTAN
CAM. CAMBODIA
Q. QATAR
UAE UNITED ARAB EMIRATES
NORTH PACIFIC OCEAN
AZER.
TURKMENIA
UZBEKISTAN
KIRGIZIA
TADZ.
NORTH KOREA
SOUTH KOREA
JAPAN
C H I N A
IRAN
AFGHANISTAN
PAKISTAN
Q.
KUWAIT
BA.
SAUDI ARABIA
UAE
OMAN
NEPAL
BH.
BD.
INDIA
BURMA
LAOS
VIETNAM
TAIWAN
HONG KONG
PHILIPPINES
THAILAND
CAM.
ASIA
YEMEN
Laccadive Is (India)
Socotra (Yemen)
SRI LANKA
MALDIVES
BRUNEI
MALAYSIA
SEYCHELLES
INDONESIA
PAPUA NEW GUINEA
30°
Midway Is
HAWAII (USA)
Tropic of Cancer
Hawaii
Marcus I (Japan)
Wake I (USA)
Mariana Is (USA)
Guam (USA)
Johnston Atoll (USA)
Marshall Is (USA)
Caroline Is (USA)
Gilbert Islands
Line Is
Equator
0°
KIRIBATI
Phoenix Islands
Tokelau Is (NZ)
SOLOMON ISLANDS
TUVALU
WESTERN SAMOA
AMERICAN SAMOA
Marquesas
Tuamotu Archipelago
COMOROS
INDIAN OCEAN
MAURITIUS
Réunion (Fr)
MADAGASCAR
Keeling Is (Aust)
Christmas I. (Aust)
VANUATU
FIJI
New Caledonia (Fr)
TONGA
Niue (NZ)
Cook Is (NZ)
FRENCH POLYNESIA
Tropic of Capricorn
A U S T R A L I A
AUSTRALASIA
30°
Kermadec Is (NZ)
ARM. ARMENIA
AZER. AZERBAIJAN
GEO. GEORGIA
TADZ. TADZHIKISTAN
St Paul I (Fr)
Crozet Is (Fr)
NEW ZEALAND
SOUTH PACIFIC OCEAN
Chatham Is (NZ)
Kerguelen I (Fr)
Heard I (Aust)
One centimetre on this map is the same as 1000 kilometres on the ground.
0 1 2
Macquarie I (Aust)
150°
Drawing the world on a flat map distorts distances. The scale line is only accurate at the Equator
180°
60°
60° 90° ANTARCTICA 120° 150°

Population growth

Improvements in food production and in health care mean that fewer children die and adults live longer. As a result the Earth's population is rising rapidly.

1920 1 800 million
1930 2 000 million
1940 2 200 million
1950 2 500 million
1960 3 000 million
1970 3 600 million
1980 4 400 million
1990 5 250 million

WORLD Physical

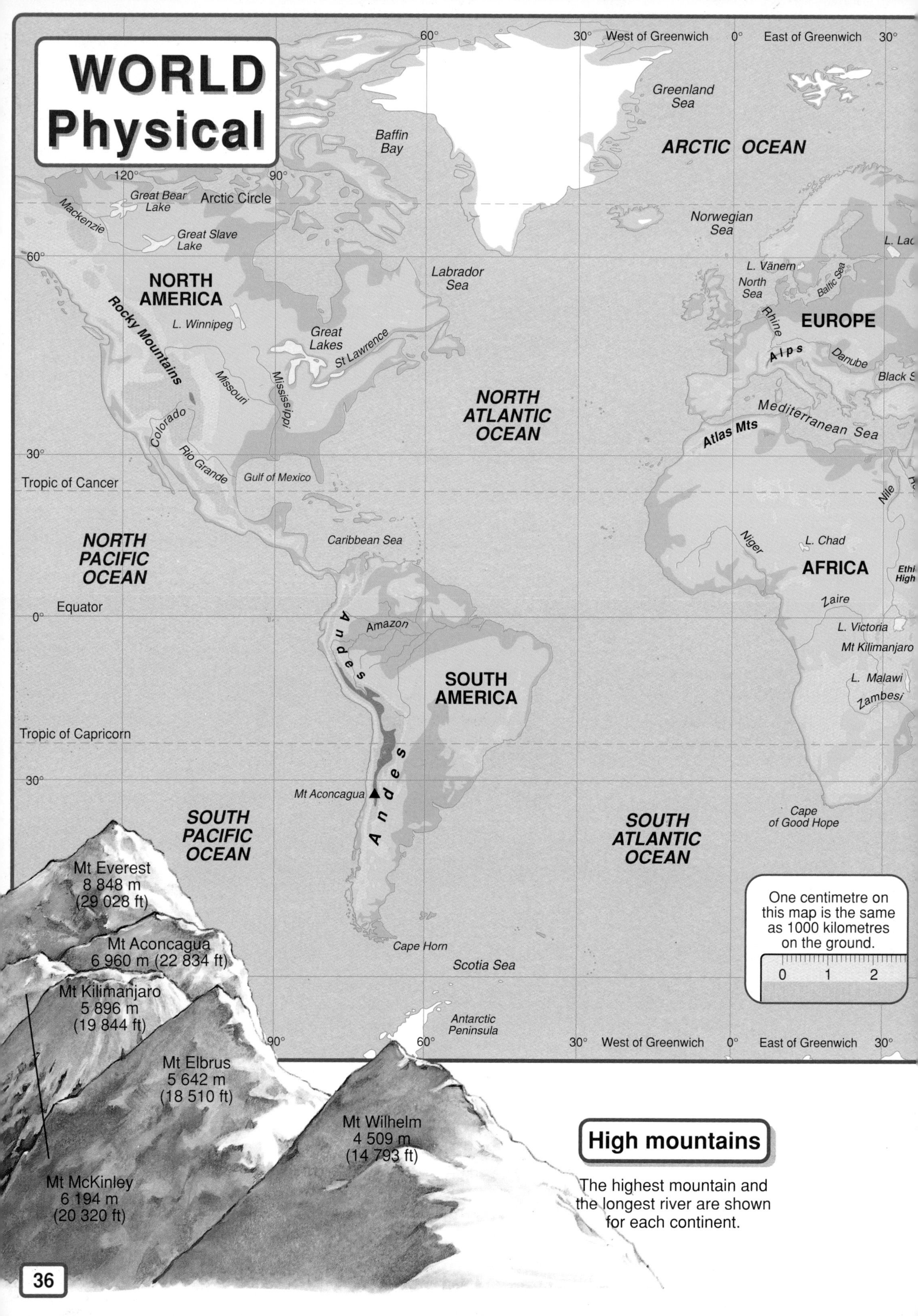

60°
30°
West of Greenwich
0°
East of Greenwich
30°
Greenland Sea
Baffin Bay
ARCTIC OCEAN
120°
90°
Great Bear Lake
Arctic Circle
Mackenzie
Great Slave Lake
Norwegian Sea
L. Lac
60°
NORTH AMERICA
Rocky Mountains
Labrador Sea
L. Vänern
North Sea
Baltic Sea
Rhine
EUROPE
L. Winnipeg
Great Lakes
St Lawrence
Alps
Danube
Black S
Missouri
Mississippi
NORTH ATLANTIC OCEAN
Mediterranean Sea
Colorado
Atlas Mts
30°
Rio Grande
Tropic of Cancer
Gulf of Mexico
Nile
Caribbean Sea
Niger
L. Chad
NORTH PACIFIC OCEAN
AFRICA
Ethi High
Equator
Zaire
0°
Andes
Amazon
L. Victoria
Mt Kilimanjaro
SOUTH AMERICA
L. Malawi
Zambesi
Tropic of Capricorn
30°
Mt Aconcagua
Cape of Good Hope
SOUTH PACIFIC OCEAN
SOUTH ATLANTIC OCEAN
One centimetre on this map is the same as 1000 kilometres on the ground.
0
1
2
Cape Horn
Scotia Sea
Antarctic Peninsula
90°
60°
30°
West of Greenwich
0°
East of Greenwich
30°
Mt Everest 8 848 m (29 028 ft)
Mt Aconcagua 6 960 m (22 834 ft)
Mt Kilimanjaro 5 896 m (19 844 ft)
Mt Elbrus 5 642 m (18 510 ft)
Mt Wilhelm 4 509 m (14 793 ft)
Mt McKinley 6 194 m (20 320 ft)

High mountains

The highest mountain and the longest river are shown for each continent.

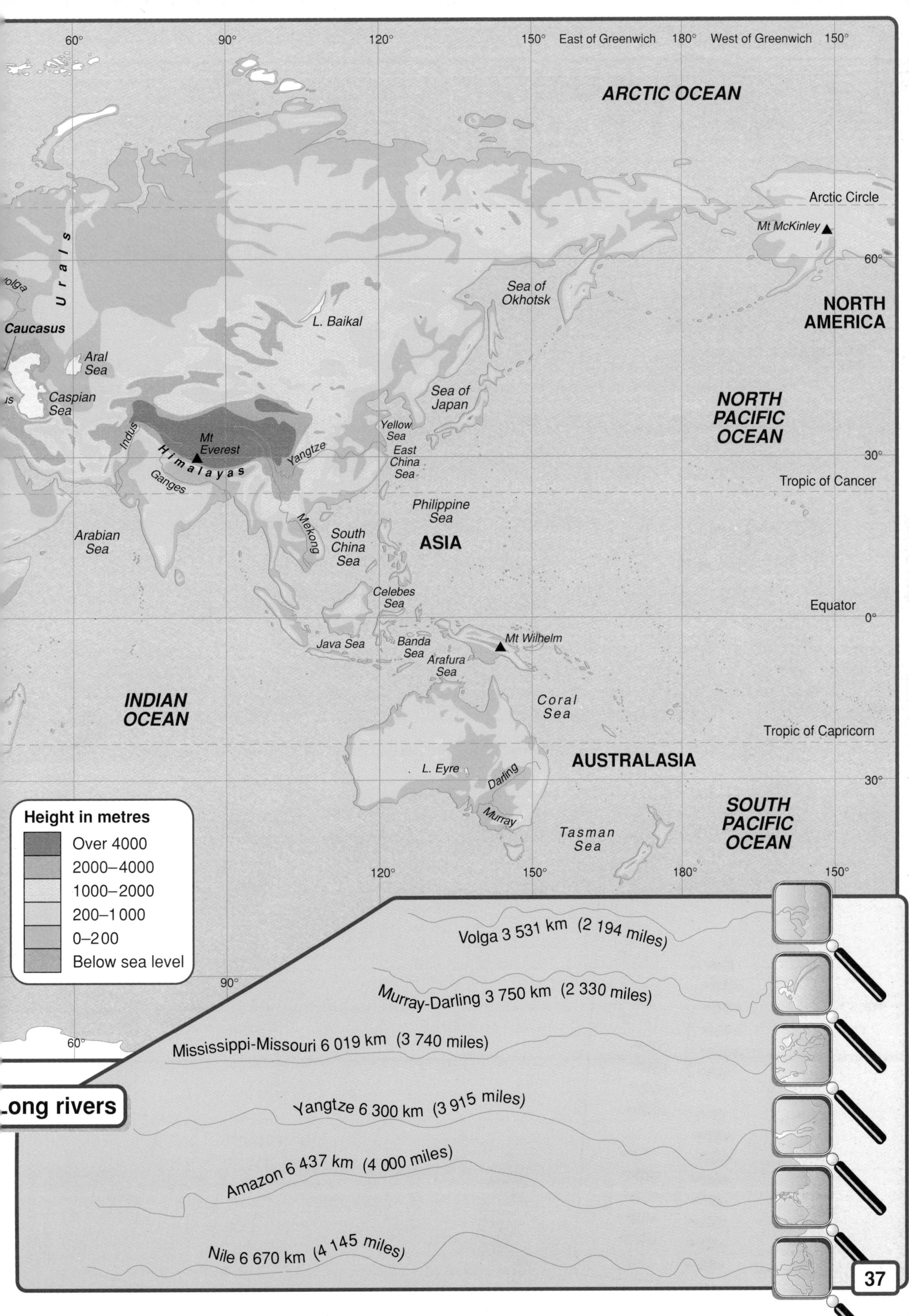

60°
90°
120°
150°
East of Greenwich
180°
West of Greenwich
150°
ARCTIC OCEAN
Arctic Circle
Mt McKinley
60°
NORTH AMERICA
Urals
Caucasus
L. Baikal
Sea of Okhotsk
Aral Sea
Caspian Sea
Sea of Japan
NORTH PACIFIC OCEAN
Indus
Mt Everest
Himalayas
Yangtze
Yellow Sea
East China Sea
Ganges
30°
Tropic of Cancer
Philippine Sea
Mekong
Arabian Sea
South China Sea
ASIA
Celebes Sea
Equator
0°
Java Sea
Banda Sea
Mt Wilhelm
Arafura Sea
INDIAN OCEAN
Coral Sea
Tropic of Capricorn
L. Eyre
Darling
AUSTRALASIA
30°
Murray
Tasman Sea
SOUTH PACIFIC OCEAN
120°
150°
180°
150°
Height in metres
Over 4000
2000–4000
1000–2000
200–1 000
0–200
Below sea level
90°
60°
Long rivers
Volga 3 531 km (2 194 miles)
Murray-Darling 3 750 km (2 330 miles)
Mississippi-Missouri 6 019 km (3 740 miles)
Yangtze 6 300 km (3 915 miles)
Amazon 6 437 km (4 000 miles)
Nile 6 670 km (4 145 miles)

EUROPE Political

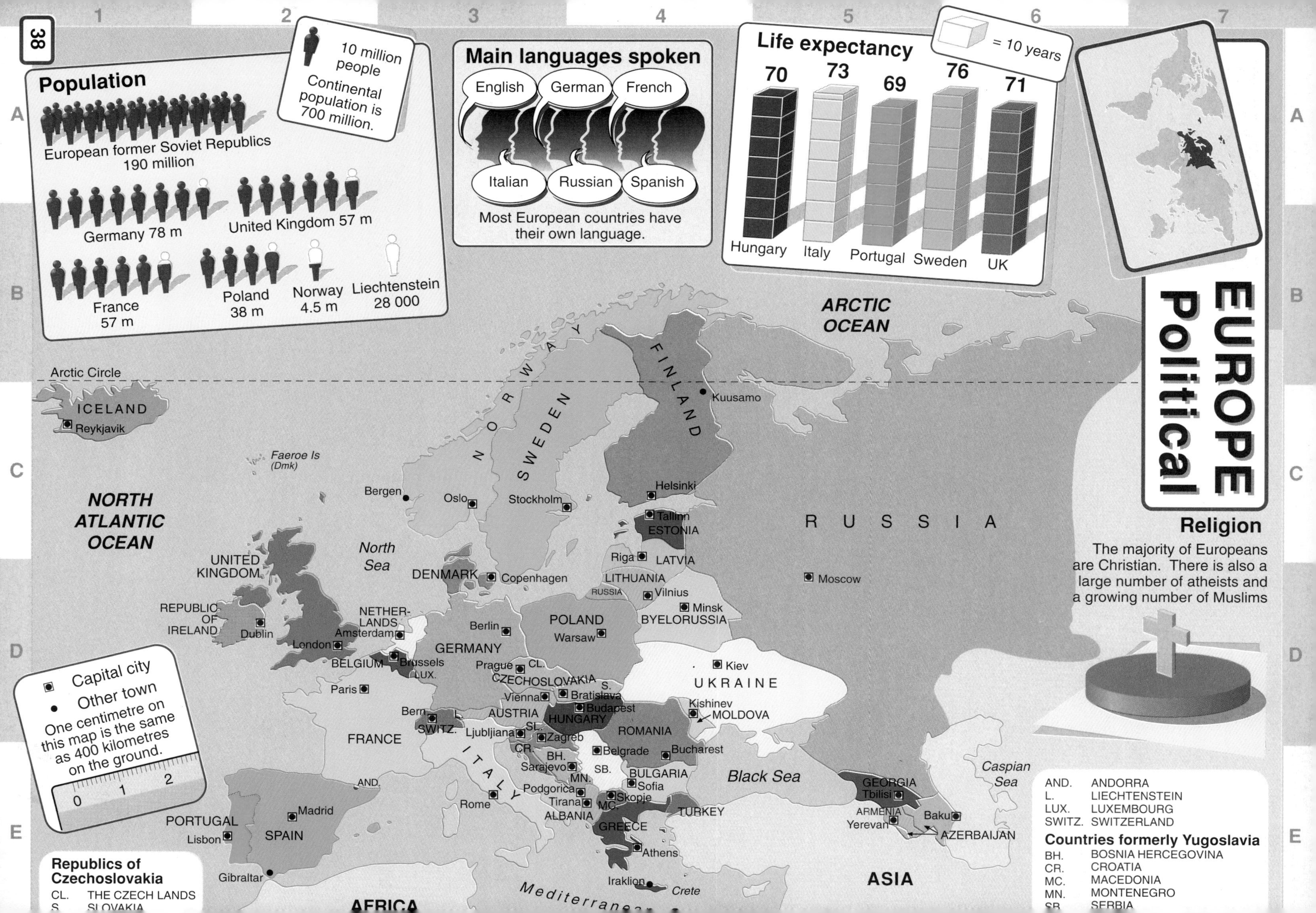

Population
European former Soviet Republics 190 million
Germany 78 m
United Kingdom 57 m
France 57 m
Poland 38 m
Norway 4.5 m
Liechtenstein 28 000
10 million people
Continental population is 700 million.
Main languages spoken
English
German
French
Italian
Russian
Spanish
Most European countries have their own language.
Life expectancy
= 10 years
70
73
69
76
71
Hungary
Italy
Portugal
Sweden
UK
Religion
The majority of Europeans are Christian. There is also a large number of atheists and a growing number of Muslims
ARCTIC OCEAN
NORTH ATLANTIC OCEAN
North Sea
Black Sea
Caspian Sea
Mediterranean
Arctic Circle
ICELAND
Reykjavik
Faeroe Is (Dmk)
NORWAY
Bergen
Oslo
SWEDEN
Stockholm
FINLAND
Kuusamo
Helsinki
Tallinn
ESTONIA
Riga
LATVIA
LITHUANIA
RUSSIA
Vilnius
Minsk
BYELORUSSIA
RUSSIA
Moscow
UNITED KINGDOM
REPUBLIC OF IRELAND
Dublin
London
DENMARK
Copenhagen
NETHER-LANDS
Amsterdam
BELGIUM
Brussels
LUX.
GERMANY
Berlin
POLAND
Warsaw
Prague
CL.
CZECHOSLOVAKIA
S.
Vienna
Bratislava
AUSTRIA
Budapest
HUNGARY
Kiev
UKRAINE
Kishinev
MOLDOVA
ROMANIA
Bucharest
Paris
FRANCE
Bern
L.
SWITZ.
Ljubljana
SL.
Zagreb
CR.
BH.
Sarajevo
Belgrade
SB.
MN.
BULGARIA
Sofia
ITALY
Rome
Podgorica
Tirana
ALBANIA
Skopje
MC.
GREECE
Athens
Iraklion
Crete
TURKEY
GEORGIA
Tbilisi
ARMENIA
Yerevan
Baku
AZERBAIJAN
ASIA
AFRICA
AND.
PORTUGAL
Lisbon
SPAIN
Madrid
Gibraltar
Capital city
Other town
One centimetre on this map is the same as 400 kilometres on the ground.
0
1
2

Republics of Czechoslovakia

CL.	THE CZECH LANDS
S.	SLOVAKIA

AND.	ANDORRA
L.	LIECHTENSTEIN
LUX.	LUXEMBOURG
SWITZ.	SWITZERLAND

Countries formerly Yugoslavia

BH.	BOSNIA HERCEGOVINA
CR.	CROATIA
MC.	MACEDONIA
MN.	MONTENEGRO
SB.	SERBIA

EUROPE Physical

Europe's climate ranges from the cold of the Arctic to the warmth of the Mediterranean.

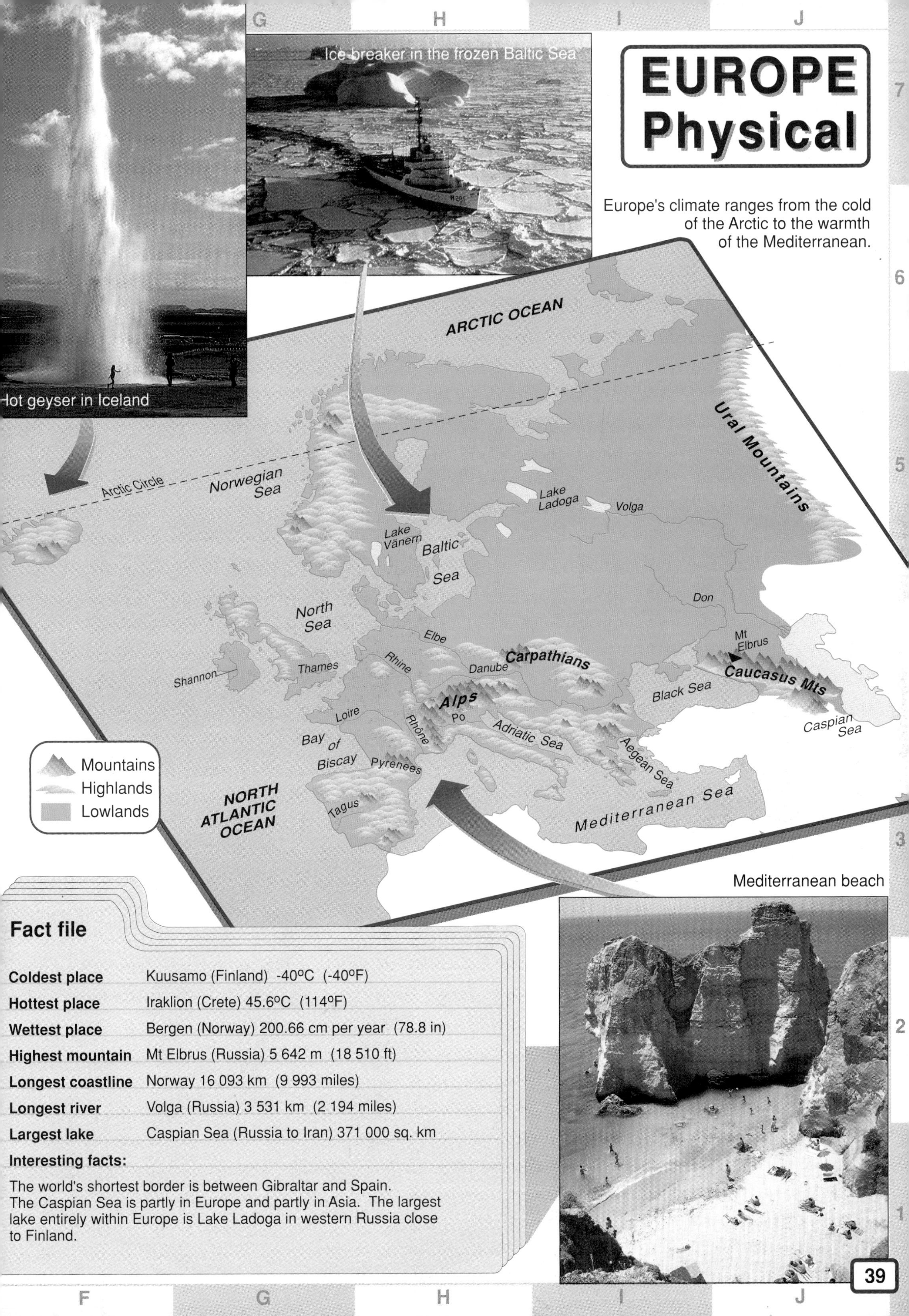
G
H
I
J
F
7
6
5
3
2
1
ARCTIC OCEAN
Arctic Circle
Norwegian Sea
Ural Mountains
Lake Ladoga
Volga
Lake Vänern
Baltic Sea
North Sea
Don
Mt Elbrus
Elbe
Rhine
Thames
Shannon
Danube
Carpathians
Caucasus Mts
Black Sea
Alps
Po
Loire
Rhône
Adriatic Sea
Aegean Sea
Caspian Sea
Bay of Biscay
Pyrenees
Tagus
NORTH ATLANTIC OCEAN
Mediterranean Sea
Mountains
Highlands
Lowlands

Ice-breaker in the frozen Baltic Sea

Hot geyser in Iceland

Mediterranean beach

Fact file

Coldest place	Kuusamo (Finland) -40°C (-40°F)
Hottest place	Iraklion (Crete) 45.6°C (114°F)
Wettest place	Bergen (Norway) 200.66 cm per year (78.8 in)
Highest mountain	Mt Elbrus (Russia) 5 642 m (18 510 ft)
Longest coastline	Norway 16 093 km (9 993 miles)
Longest river	Volga (Russia) 3 531 km (2 194 miles)
Largest lake	Caspian Sea (Russia to Iran) 371 000 sq. km

Interesting facts:

The world's shortest border is between Gibraltar and Spain. The Caspian Sea is partly in Europe and partly in Asia. The largest lake entirely within Europe is Lake Ladoga in western Russia close to Finland.

EUROPE Global Issues

Acid rain

Acid rain is formed when pollution from power stations, factories and vehicles rises into the air and mixes with raindrops. The wind blows the rainclouds. The acid rain often falls far away from the area where the pollution was created. Acid rain affects streams and lakes. Many become so polluted that fish life is completely destroyed. Forests too are being badly damaged by acid rain. In Europe the polluted air is blown by the SW winds and causes damage in northern Europe and Scandinavia.

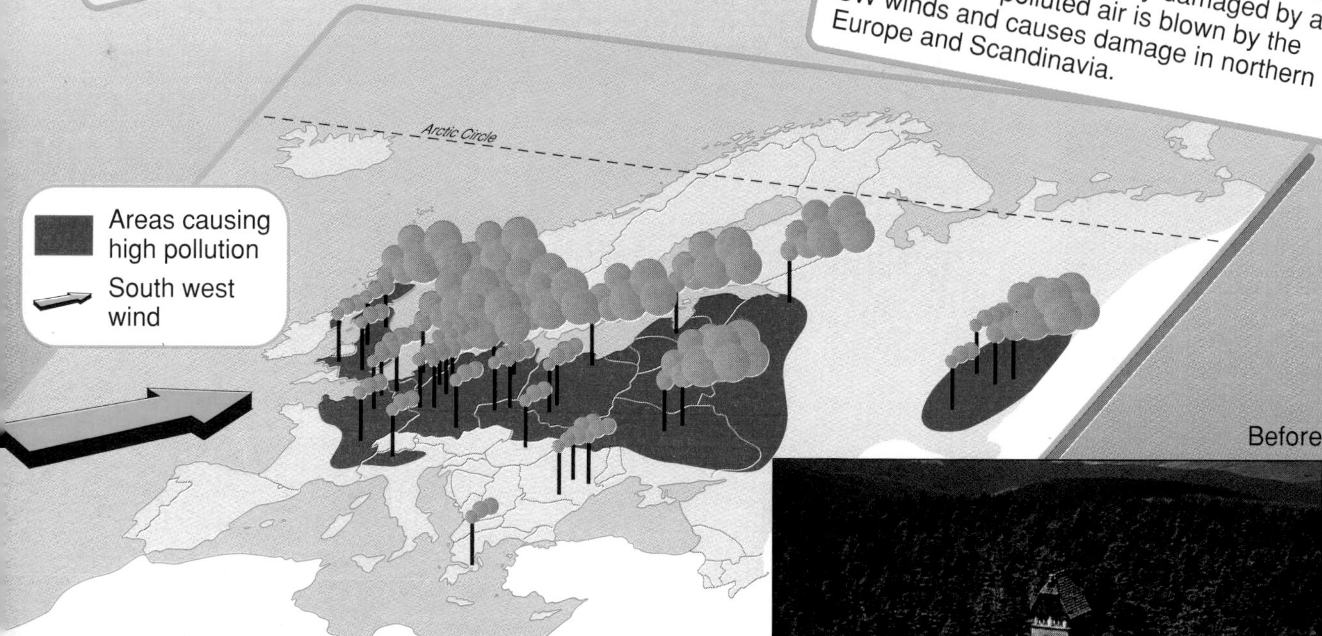

Arctic Circle

Areas causing high pollution

South west wind

Before

15 years lat

Industrial pollution

Polluted clouds

Environmental damage

Acid rain

Fish killed by pollution

Gasping for air

Crisis in Athens

During the summer the air in Athens can be so bad that people die. Athens has grown rapidly this century. Millions of people have moved there. On a hot day fumes from factories and from the large number of old cars stuck in the traffic jams poison the air. If there is no wind to blow the foul air away it simply gets worse and worse. This not only affects the people. Many of the magnificent ancient buildings of Athens are being damaged by air pollution.

When conditions are really bad the Mayor of Athens has to take emergency action. Sometimes only cars with four passengers are allowed into the city. There are even days when all cars have been banned from Athens. Other cities around the world have he same problem. In many of them nasks are worn to reduce the effects of the poisonous air.

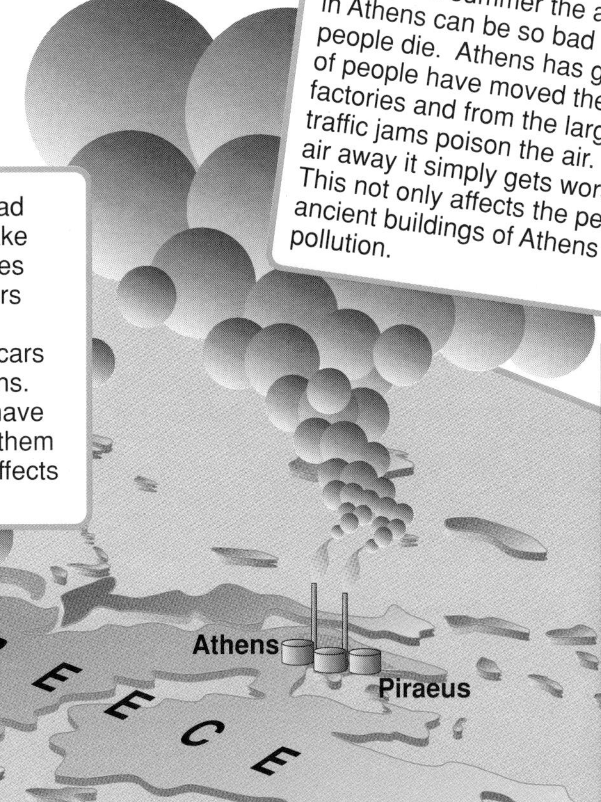

GREECE

Athens

Piraeus

Parthenon, Athens

thens

As people in the rich world grow richer many families own two or three cars. As standards of living improve in the economically developing world more and more cars will be bought and driven. What other types of transport will need to be available in large cities if people are to leave their cars at home?

World of cars

The picture shows the number of cars compared with the size of the population. For example, for every 100 people in the USA there are more than 50 cars; in China there is fewer than 1 car for every 100 people.

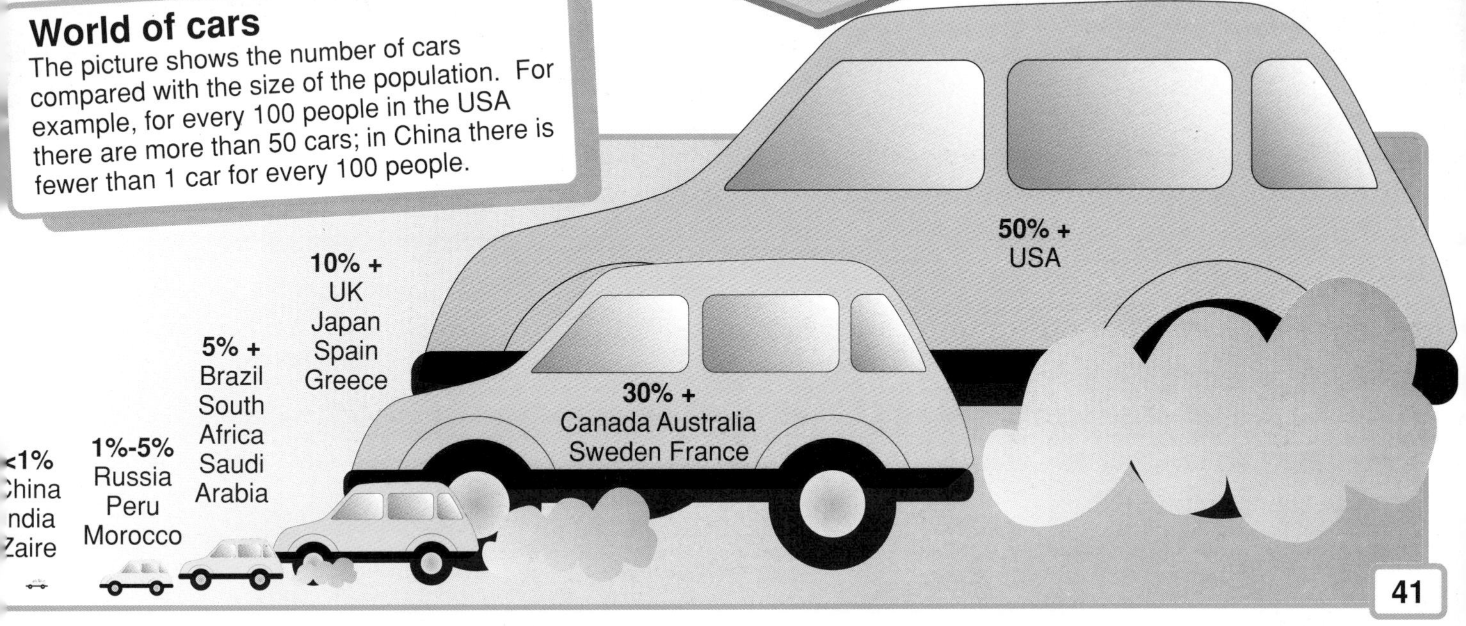

50% + USA

30% + Canada Australia Sweden France

10% + UK Japan Spain Greece

5% + Brazil South Africa Saudi Arabia

1%-5% Russia Peru Morocco

<1% China India Zaire

ASIA Political

The variety of languages, cultures, dress, diet, homes and lifestyles is enormous. The old and new exist side by side. Many different alphabets are in use across Asia.

Asia contains the countries with the world's highest populations. China already has more than 1 000 million people. India too will reach 1 000 million by the year 2000.

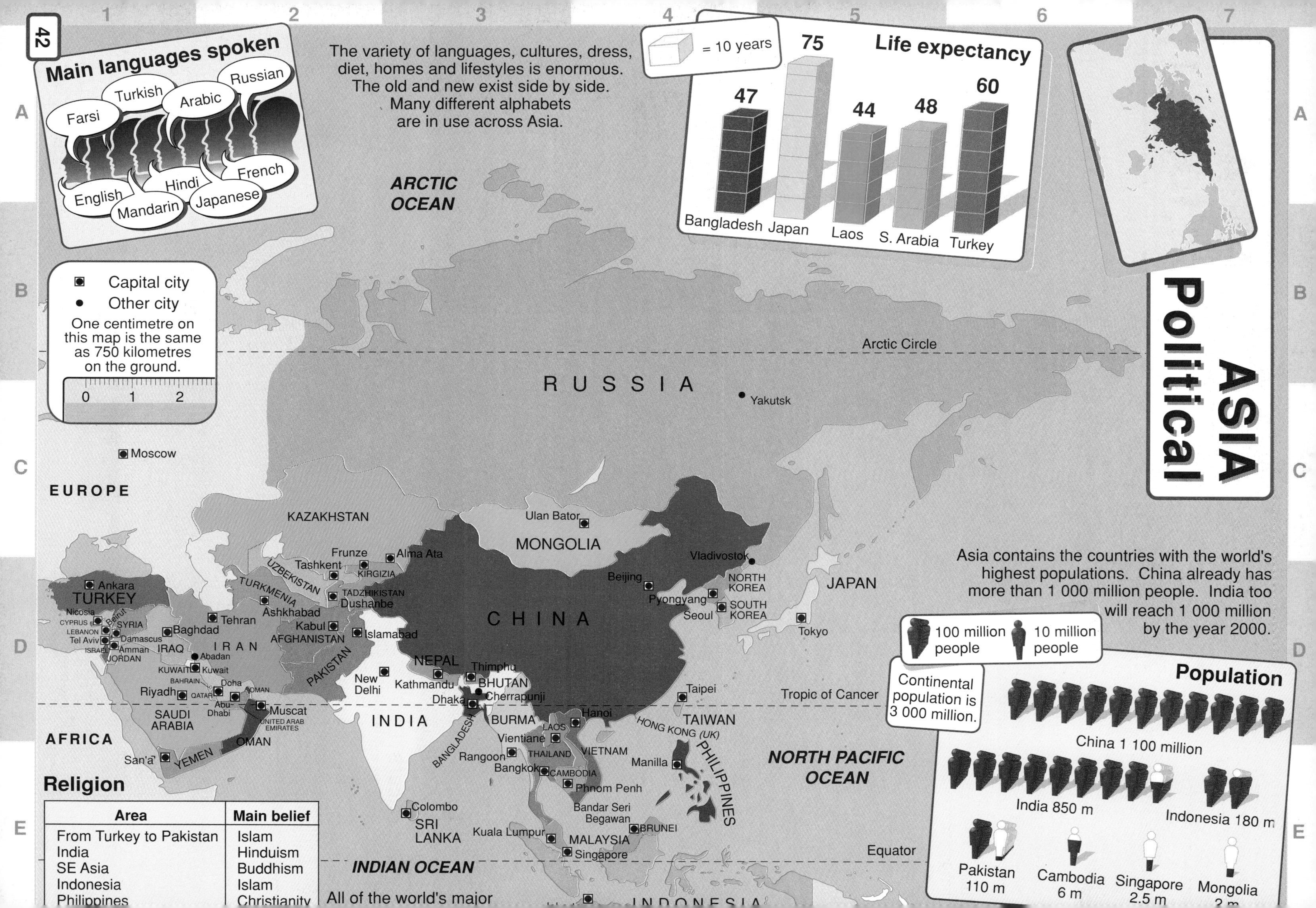

Main languages spoken
Farsi
Turkish
Arabic
Russian
English
Mandarin
Hindi
Japanese
French
Life expectancy
= 10 years
47
75
44
48
60
Bangladesh
Japan
Laos
S. Arabia
Turkey
Capital city
Other city
One centimetre on this map is the same as 750 kilometres on the ground.
0
1
2
ARCTIC OCEAN
Arctic Circle
RUSSIA
Yakutsk
Moscow
EUROPE
KAZAKHSTAN
Ulan Bator
MONGOLIA
Frunze
Alma Ata
Tashkent
KIRGIZIA
UZBEKISTAN
TURKMENIA
TADZHIKISTAN
Dushanbe
Ashkhabad
Ankara
TURKEY
Nicosia
CYPRUS
Beirut
SYRIA
LEBANON
Tel Aviv
ISRAEL
Damascus
Amman
JORDAN
Baghdad
IRAQ
Tehran
IRAN
Abadan
KUWAIT
Kuwait
BAHRAIN
Doha
QATAR
Riyadh
SAUDI ARABIA
Abu-Dhabi
OMAN
Muscat
UNITED ARAB EMIRATES
OMAN
San'a'
YEMEN
AFRICA
Kabul
AFGHANISTAN
Islamabad
PAKISTAN
New Delhi
Kathmandu
NEPAL
Thimphu
BHUTAN
Cherrapunji
Dhaka
BANGLADESH
INDIA
Colombo
SRI LANKA
CHINA
Beijing
Vladivostok
NORTH KOREA
Pyongyang
Seoul
SOUTH KOREA
JAPAN
Tokyo
Taipei
TAIWAN
HONG KONG (UK)
PHILIPPINES
Manilla
Tropic of Cancer
BURMA
Rangoon
LAOS
Vientiane
Hanoi
VIETNAM
THAILAND
Bangkok
CAMBODIA
Phnom Penh
Bandar Seri Begawan
BRUNEI
Kuala Lumpur
MALAYSIA
Singapore
INDONESIA
NORTH PACIFIC OCEAN
INDIAN OCEAN
Equator
100 million people
10 million people
Continental population is 3 000 million.
Population
China 1 100 million
India 850 m
Indonesia 180 m
Pakistan 110 m
Cambodia 6 m
Singapore 2.5 m
Mongolia 2 m

Religion

Area	Main belief
From Turkey to Pakistan	Islam
India	Hinduism
SE Asia	Buddhism
Indonesia	Islam
Philippines	Christianity

All of the world's major

ASIA Physical

…e climates of Asia range from …e extreme cold of Arctic Russia …the intense heat of equatorial …donesia.

F
G
H
I
J
7
6
4
3
Taiga
Arabian Desert
ARCTIC OCEAN
Ural Mts
Siberia
Steppes
Aral Sea
Caspian Sea
Lake Baikal
Arctic Circle
Tian Shan
Altai
Gobi Desert
Arabian Desert
Persian Gulf
Indus
Himalayas
Mt Everest
Ganges
Brahmaputra
Yangtze
Arabian Sea
Bay of Bengal
Mekong
Sea of Japan
NORTH PACIFIC OCEAN
South China Sea
Philippine Sea
Tropic of Cancer
INDIAN OCEAN
Sumatera
Borneo
Equator
Mountains
Highlands
Lowlands
Deserts
Mount Everest

Fact file

Coldest place	Yakutsk (Russia) -64.3ºC (-84ºF)
Hottest place	Abadan (Iran) 52.8ºC (127ºF)
Wettest place	Cherrapunji (India) 1 079.5 cm per year (425.1 in)
Highest mountain	Mt Everest (Nepal/China) 8 848 m (29 028 ft)
Longest coastline	Indonesia 54 716 km (33 978 miles)
Longest river	Yangtze *[Chang Jiang]* (China) 6 300 km (3 915 miles)
Largest lake	Caspian Sea (Russia to Iran) 371 000 sq. km (143 205 sq. miles)

Interesting facts:

Asia is the world's largest continent; it covers almost one third of the world's land surface.
60% of the world's population live in Asia.
The world's longest railway is the Trans-Siberian which is 9 438 km (5 864 miles) long and links Moscow with Vladivostok.

ASIA Global Issues

The problem

Housing and feeding a growing population is not easy. Different countries try different methods of dealing with this challenge.

Population growth

The growth of the world's population leads to an increased demand on food and other resources. Europe had its rapid population growth in the last century. Today growth is greatest in Asia, Africa, Central and South America.

China: The response

In China people are not allowed to move from the countryside to the city without permission. This is to avoid large numbers of homeless people living in shanty towns. Parents in most of China are expected to have only one child.

Indonesia: The response

Indonesia is a country of many islands. Peop from the main islands such as Jawa are giv land in other parts of Indone including Timor a Irian Ja

CHINA
Tropic of Cancer
Equator
INDONESIA
Irian Jaya
Jawa
Timor

One problem now facing China is that of spoilt children. Grandparents, parents and relatives give so much time and attention to the only child that many now have the nickname 'The Little Emperor'.

'Freedom fighters' - East Timor

The native people of Timor and Irian Jaya have seen their forests destroyed to provid land for the new settlers. Today many natives, whos families have lived there fo generations, are fighting th Indonesian government an demanding independence and an end to the settlements.

Natural disasters

Many parts of the world around the tropics depend on heavy rain for the crops to grow. This rain is *seasonal* and is known as the *Monsoon.* The monsoon should mean good news for the farmers but sometimes it means disaster.

Monsoon areas of the world

As summer comes to monsoon areas the land warms up. The air above it rises and fresh air is drawn from over the ocean. This air is heavy with water which has evaporated from the sea. Clouds travel and pass over the land where they drop enormous quantities of rain. In South Asia the wind carries moisture from the Indian Ocean to the surrounding land.

A hurricane develops

Sometimes the monsoon can turn into a hurricane. A hurricane spins as it crosses the ocean. It collects more and more rain as it travels. Hurricane force winds develop. Giant waves are formed. They can destroy everything on low lying land.

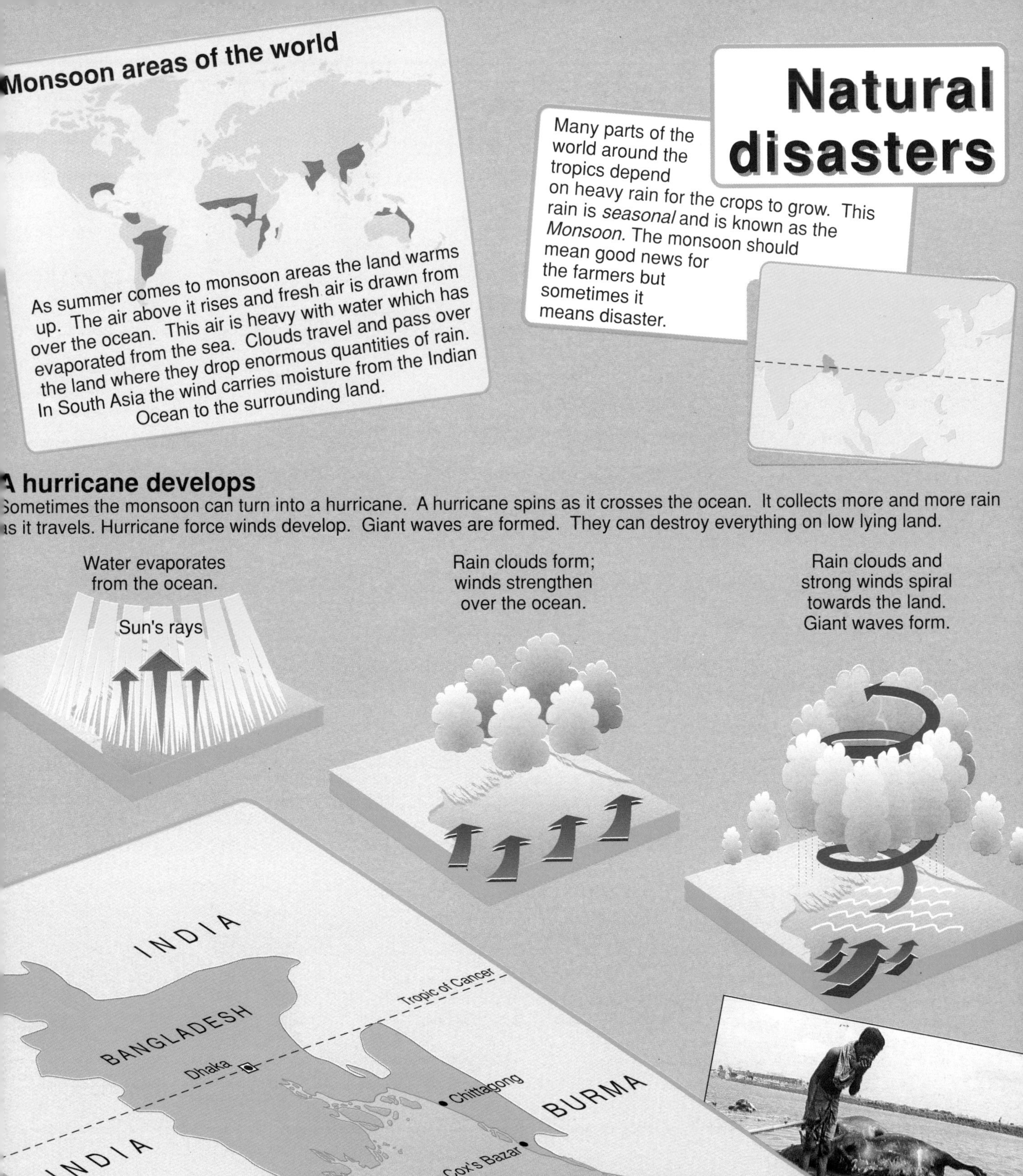
Water evaporates from the ocean.
Sun's rays
Rain clouds form; winds strengthen over the ocean.
Rain clouds and strong winds spiral towards the land. Giant waves form.
INDIA
Tropic of Cancer
BANGLADESH
Dhaka
Chittagong
BURMA
INDIA
Cox's Bazar
Bay of Bengal
INDIAN OCEAN

Bangladesh is in the path of such hurricanes. The coast is very low, flat and exposed. When the hurricane arrives it can destroy everything in its path.

Effect of the 1991 hurricane on Bangladesh.

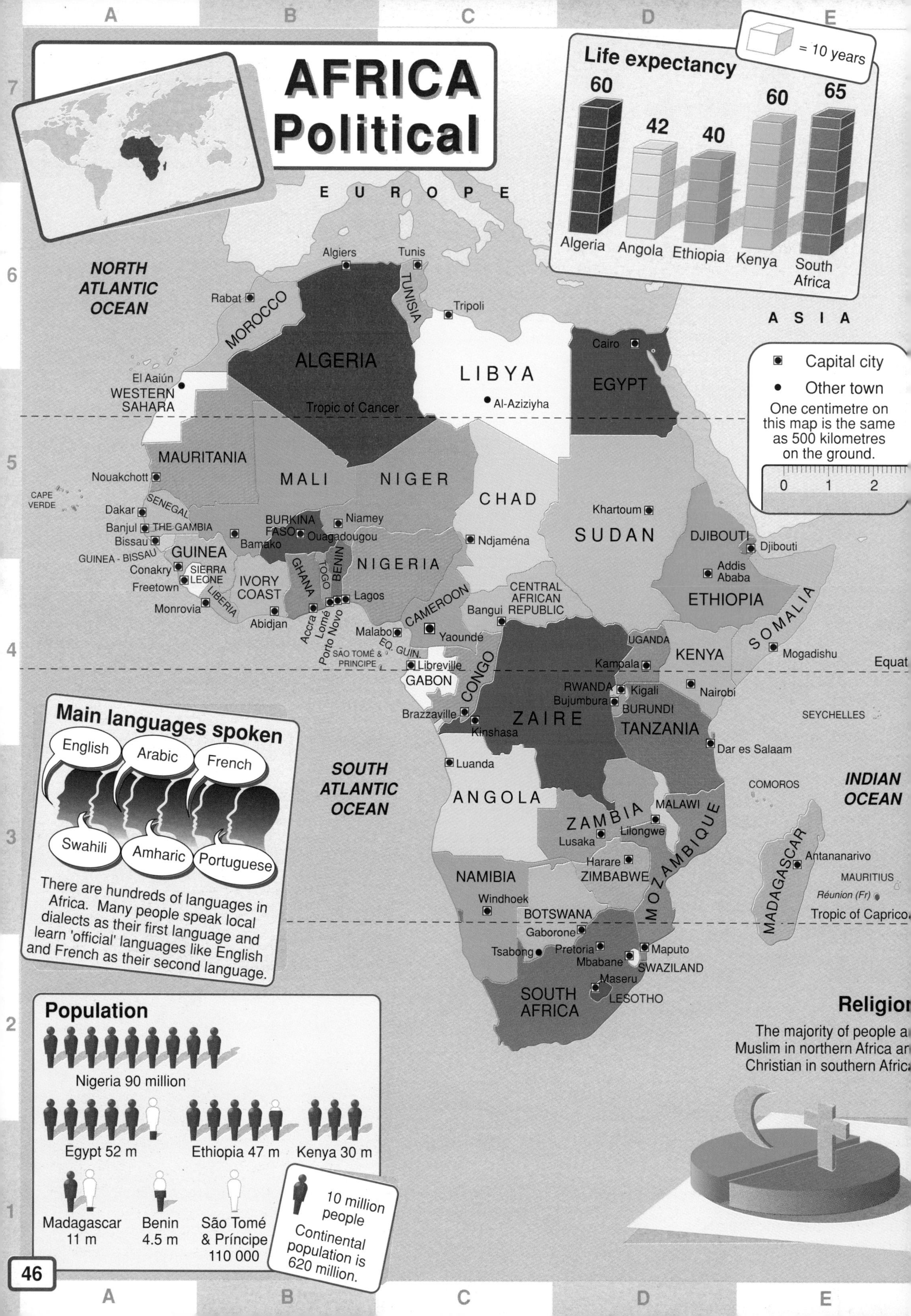

AFRICA
Political
Life expectancy
= 10 years
60
Algeria
42
Angola
40
Ethiopia
60
Kenya
65
South Africa
E U R O P E
A S I A
NORTH ATLANTIC OCEAN
SOUTH ATLANTIC OCEAN
INDIAN OCEAN
Capital city
Other town
One centimetre on this map is the same as 500 kilometres on the ground.
0
1
2
Algiers
Tunis
Rabat
Tripoli
MOROCCO
TUNISIA
ALGERIA
LIBYA
Cairo
EGYPT
El Aaiún
WESTERN SAHARA
Al-Aziziyha
Tropic of Cancer
MAURITANIA
Nouakchott
MALI
NIGER
CHAD
CAPE VERDE
Dakar
SENEGAL
Banjul
THE GAMBIA
Bissau
GUINEA - BISSAU
GUINEA
Conakry
SIERRA LEONE
Freetown
LIBERIA
Monrovia
IVORY COAST
Abidjan
Bamako
BURKINA FASO
Ouagadougou
Niamey
GHANA
TOGO
BENIN
Accra
Lomé
Porto Novo
Lagos
NIGERIA
Ndjaména
Khartoum
SUDAN
DJIBOUTI
Djibouti
Addis Ababa
ETHIOPIA
SOMALIA
Mogadishu
CAMEROON
Yaounde
Malabo
EQ. GUIN.
SÃO TOMÉ & PRINCIPE
Libreville
GABON
CONGO
Brazzaville
Kinshasa
CENTRAL AFRICAN REPUBLIC
Bangui
ZAIRE
UGANDA
Kampala
KENYA
Nairobi
RWANDA
Kigali
Bujumbura
BURUNDI
TANZANIA
Dar es Salaam
Equat
SEYCHELLES
COMOROS
Luanda
ANGOLA
ZAMBIA
Lusaka
MALAWI
Lilongwe
MOZAMBIQUE
Harare
ZIMBABWE
NAMIBIA
Windhoek
BOTSWANA
Gaborone
Tsabong
Pretoria
Mbabane
Maputo
SWAZILAND
Maseru
LESOTHO
SOUTH AFRICA
MADAGASCAR
Antananarivo
MAURITIUS
Réunion (Fr)
Tropic of Caprico
Main languages spoken
English
Arabic
French
Swahili
Amharic
Portuguese
There are hundreds of languages in Africa. Many people speak local dialects as their first language and learn 'official' languages like English and French as their second language.
Population
Nigeria 90 million
Egypt 52 m
Ethiopia 47 m
Kenya 30 m
Madagascar 11 m
Benin 4.5 m
São Tomé & Príncipe 110 000
10 million people
Continental population is 620 million.
Religio
The majority of people a Muslim in northern Africa ar Christian in southern Afric
A
B
C
D
E
7
6
5
4
3
2
1

AFRICA Physical

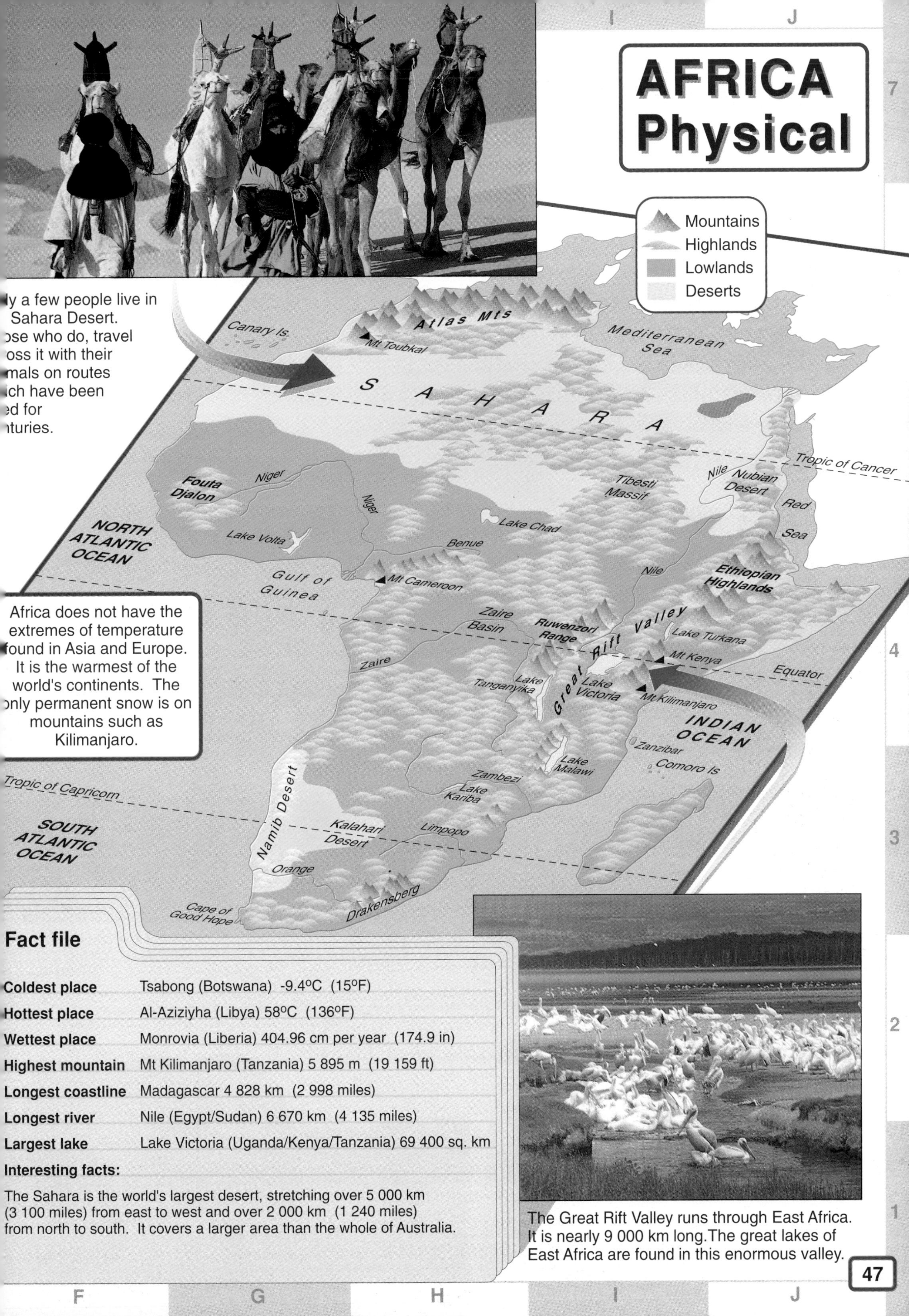

Mountains
Highlands
Lowlands
Deserts
Canary Is.
Atlas Mts
Mt Toubkal
Mediterranean Sea
S A H A R A
Tropic of Cancer
Nile
Nubian Desert
Red Sea
Tibesti Massif
Fouta Djalon
Niger
Niger
Lake Chad
NORTH ATLANTIC OCEAN
Lake Volta
Benue
Gulf of Guinea
Mt Cameroon
Nile
Ethiopian Highlands
Zaire Basin
Ruwenzori Range
Great Rift Valley
Lake Turkana
Mt Kenya
Zaire
Equator
Lake Tanganyika
Lake Victoria
Mt Kilimanjaro
INDIAN OCEAN
Zanzibar
Comoro Is
Lake Malawi
Zambezi
Tropic of Capricorn
Namib Desert
Lake Kariba
SOUTH ATLANTIC OCEAN
Kalahari Desert
Limpopo
Orange
Drakensberg
Cape of Good Hope
F
G
H
I
J
7
4
3
2
1

ly a few people live in Sahara Desert. ose who do, travel oss it with their mals on routes ich have been ed for nturies.

Africa does not have the extremes of temperature found in Asia and Europe. It is the warmest of the world's continents. The only permanent snow is on mountains such as Kilimanjaro.

Fact file

Coldest place	Tsabong (Botswana) -9.4°C (15°F)
Hottest place	Al-Aziziyha (Libya) 58°C (136°F)
Wettest place	Monrovia (Liberia) 404.96 cm per year (174.9 in)
Highest mountain	Mt Kilimanjaro (Tanzania) 5 895 m (19 159 ft)
Longest coastline	Madagascar 4 828 km (2 998 miles)
Longest river	Nile (Egypt/Sudan) 6 670 km (4 135 miles)
Largest lake	Lake Victoria (Uganda/Kenya/Tanzania) 69 400 sq. km

Interesting facts:

The Sahara is the world's largest desert, stretching over 5 000 km (3 100 miles) from east to west and over 2 000 km (1 240 miles) from north to south. It covers a larger area than the whole of Australia.

The Great Rift Valley runs through East Africa. It is nearly 9 000 km long.The great lakes of East Africa are found in this enormous valley.

AFRICA Global Issues

Wildlife at risk

Around the world, wildlife is under threat. Some species have already disappeared forever. Others are in danger now.

The world elephant population

Elephants in Africa

In the past

Today

Tropic of Cancer

Equator

Tropic of Capricorn

In Africa the elephant population has been shrinking rapidly. There are three main reasons:

1 More and more of the land used by people for farming. The elephants' habitat is therefore being destroyed.
2 Elephants have been killed for their ivory which can be sold for large amounts of money.
3 Changes in the climate.

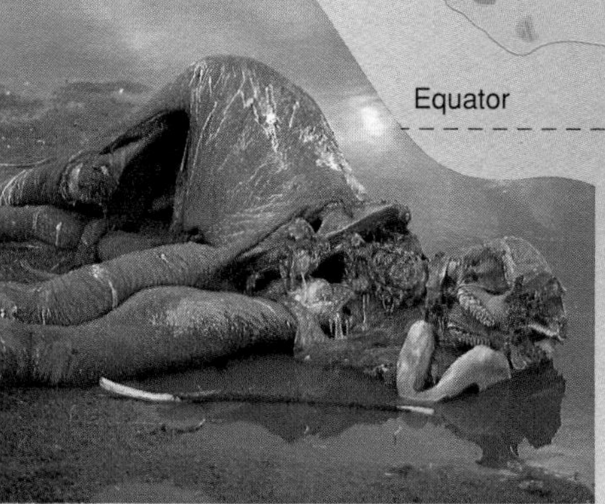

Some countries have protected the elephants by providing nature reserves, where elephant numbers are controlled but elephants can enjoy a natural existence. The nature reserves attract tourists who bring much needed money to the area.

Goods carved from ivory were once sold all around the world. Now most countries have agreed to ban the trade in ivory. When ivory is taken from poachers it is burned. This is to prevent the trade continuing.

20 years ago — 3 000 000 elephants

10 years ago — 1 300 000

Today — 600 000

? — The last elephant?

What should anyone who cares about the future of elephants do if offered the chance to buy ivory products?

Advancing deserts

The rains which used to come regularly to Ethiopia and Sudan are no longer reliable. Without the rain, crops do not grow and the natural vegetation on which animals live is also damaged.

Deserts of the World

The area of the world covered by desert is increasing.

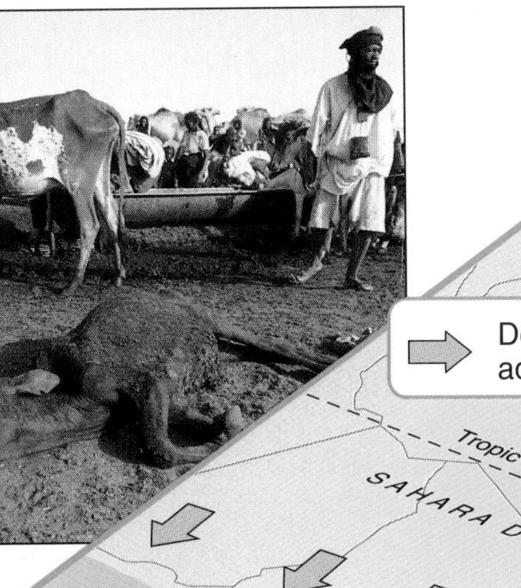

Desert advancing

Mediterranean Sea

Tropic of Cancer

SAHARA DESERT

EGYPT

Nubian Desert

SUDAN

Nile

Red Sea

Ethiopian Highlands

Addis Ababa

ETHIOPIA

INDIAN OCEAN

f the local land
s too dry the people
nd their animals move to
vhere there is water and grazing.

As the population grows more use is made of the land. More trees are chopped down for fuel, more animals graze and more forest is cleared for farming.

The extra animals eat the young trees before they can grow.

Without the trees the soil becomes loose.

The loose soil is blown away, fewer crops grow and the land turns to desert.

SOUTH AMERICA
Political
Life expectancy
= 10 years
50 Bolivia
65 Brazil
60 Ecuador
55 Peru
70 Uruguay
CENTRAL AMERICA
Religion
Almost all the people in South America are Christian.
Caracas
VENEZUELA
Georgetown
Paramaribo
Cayenne
GUYANA
SURINAM
FRENCH GUIANA
NORTH ATLANTIC OCEAN
Bogotá
COLOMBIA
Galapagos Is (Ecuador)
Quito
Andagoya
Equator
ECUADOR
PERU
BRAZIL
Lima
SOUTH ATLANTIC OCEAN
La Paz
BOLIVIA
Brasilia
Main languages spoken
Spanish
Quecha
Portuguese
PARAGUAY
São Paulo
Rio de Janeiro
Tropic of Capricorn
Asunción
Santiago del Estero
CHILE
ARGENTINA
Santiago
URUGUAY
Buenos Aires
Montevideo
Capital city
Other city
One centimetre on this map is the same as 500 kilometres on the ground.
0 1 2
PACIFIC OCEAN
Argentina attracted immigrants from many parts of Europe.
Falkland Is (UK)
Punta Arenas
Population
Brazil 136 million
Argentina 31 m
Peru 20 m
Chile 12 m
Bolivia 6 m
Uruguay 3 m
Surinam 0.5 m
10 million people
Continental population is 300 million.
Peru was once a part of the great Inca Empire. Markets like these have been held on the same sites since Inca times.
A B C D E
7 6 5 4 3 2 1

SOUTH AMERICA Physical

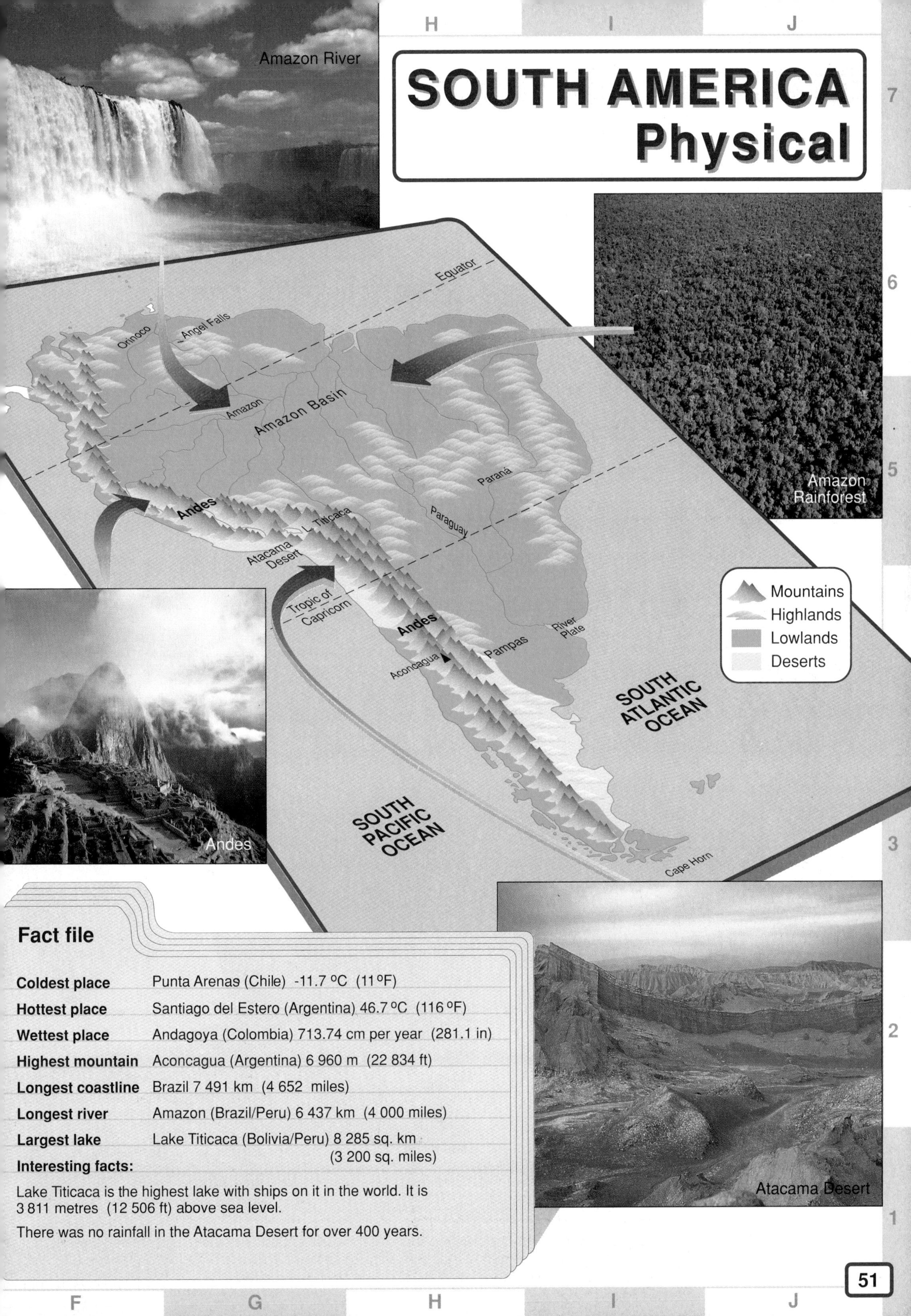

H
I
J
7
6
5
3
2
1
Amazon River
Equator
Orinoco
Angel Falls
Amazon
Amazon Basin
Paraná
Paraguay
Andes
L. Titicaca
Atacama Desert
Tropic of Capricorn
Andes
Aconcagua
Pampas
River Plate
SOUTH ATLANTIC OCEAN
SOUTH PACIFIC OCEAN
Cape Horn
Mountains
Highlands
Lowlands
Deserts
Amazon Rainforest
Andes
Atacama Desert
F
G
H
I
J

Fact file

Coldest place	Punta Arenas (Chile) -11.7 ºC (11 ºF)
Hottest place	Santiago del Estero (Argentina) 46.7 ºC (116 ºF)
Wettest place	Andagoya (Colombia) 713.74 cm per year (281.1 in)
Highest mountain	Aconcagua (Argentina) 6 960 m (22 834 ft)
Longest coastline	Brazil 7 491 km (4 652 miles)
Longest river	Amazon (Brazil/Peru) 6 437 km (4 000 miles)
Largest lake	Lake Titicaca (Bolivia/Peru) 8 285 sq. km (3 200 sq. miles)

Interesting facts:

Lake Titicaca is the highest lake with ships on it in the world. It is 3 811 metres (12 506 ft) above sea level.

There was no rainfall in the Atacama Desert for over 400 years.

SOUTH AMERICA Global Issues

Tropical rainforests of the world

The high temperatures and heavy rainfall in lowland areas around the Equator provide perfect conditions for the growth of rainforests

Rainforest
Mountains
River
One centimetre on this map is the same as 500 kilometres on the ground.
0
1
2
Orinoco
Equator
Cotopaxi
Chimborazo
Amazon
Amazon
Andes
Paraguay
Paraná
Tropic of Capricorn
Andes
Aconcagua

Yes, we cut the trees down and burn the stumps to clear the land. We farm it for 2 years then move on and the forest grows again.

Every day the world loses an area of rainforest equal to 300 000 soccer pitches. Where will it end?

I clear the forest and sell the wood. The land can be used to grow food for our city people. This provides jobs for farmers. It's not my problem that the land will be ruined; anyway there's lots more.

Value of th rainforests

Helps keep the worl climate in balance. T rainforest soaks up t heavy rainfall, some which slowly joins t rivers, and the r evaporates, rea to fall aga

Home for traditional peoples

Home for millions of species of animal, insect and plant life

Wood products

Rosy periwinkle is used in drugs to treat leukaemia.

Many new drugs are developed from rainforest plants.

The world's rainforests are disappearing fast. Governments know this but they also need the money that comes from selling hardwood, the land for people to farm, and food for the towns and cities.

City growth

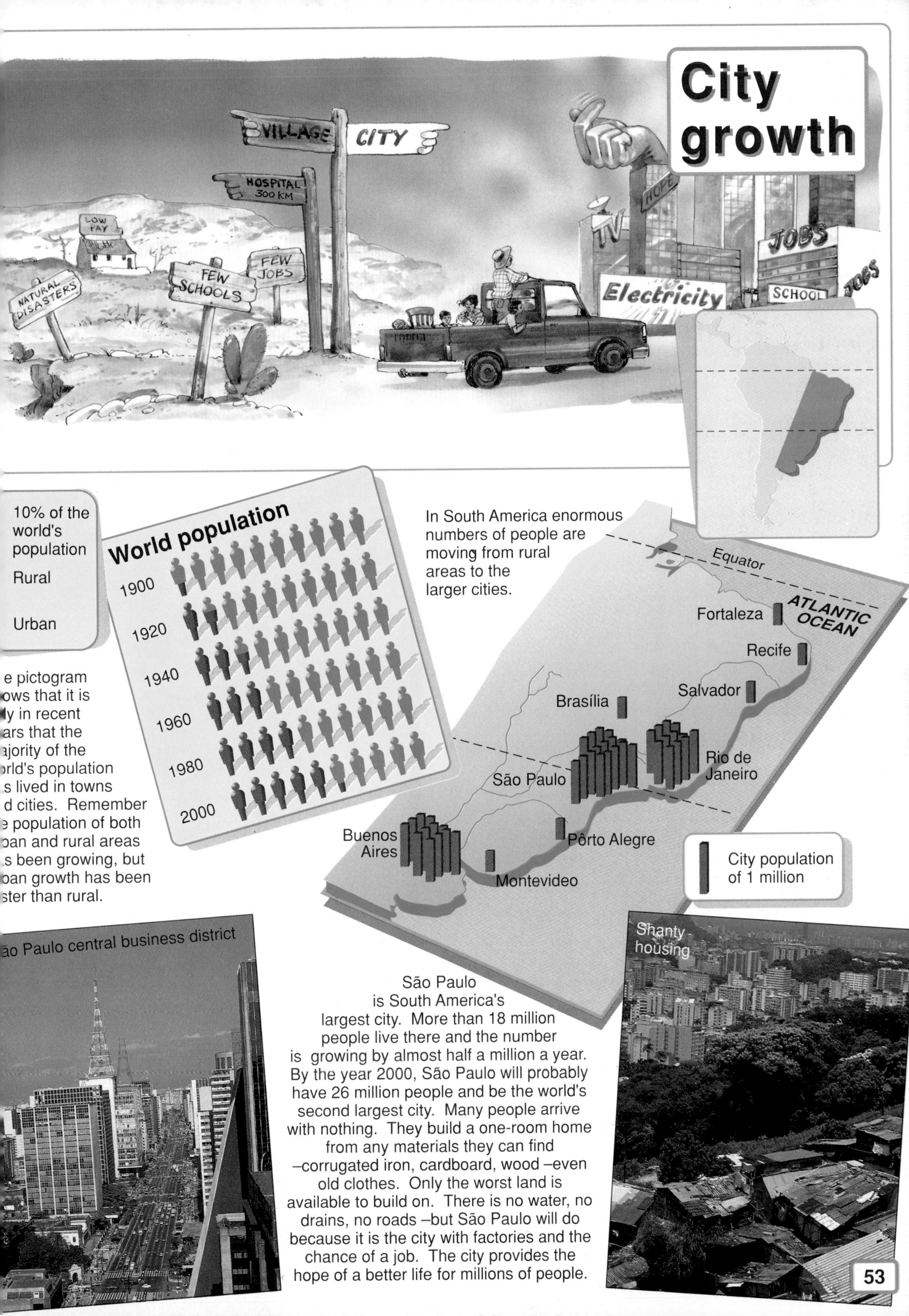

VILLAGE
CITY
HOSPITAL 300 KM
LOW PAY
NATURAL DISASTERS
FEW SCHOOLS
FEW JOBS
HOPE
TV
JOBS
Electricity
SCHOOL
JOBS
10% of the world's population
Rural
Urban
World population
1900
1920
1940
1960
1980
2000
Equator
ATLANTIC OCEAN
Fortaleza
Recife
Salvador
Brasília
Rio de Janeiro
São Paulo
Buenos Aires
Montevideo
Pôrto Alegre
City population of 1 million

In South America enormous numbers of people are moving from rural areas to the larger cities.

e pictogram ows that it is ly in recent ars that the ajority of the orld's population s lived in towns d cities. Remember e population of both oan and rural areas s been growing, but oan growth has been ster than rural.

ão Paulo central business district

Shanty housing

São Paulo is South America's largest city. More than 18 million people live there and the number is growing by almost half a million a year. By the year 2000, São Paulo will probably have 26 million people and be the world's second largest city. Many people arrive with nothing. They build a one-room home from any materials they can find –corrugated iron, cardboard, wood –even old clothes. Only the worst land is available to build on. There is no water, no drains, no roads –but São Paulo will do because it is the city with factories and the chance of a job. The city provides the hope of a better life for millions of people.

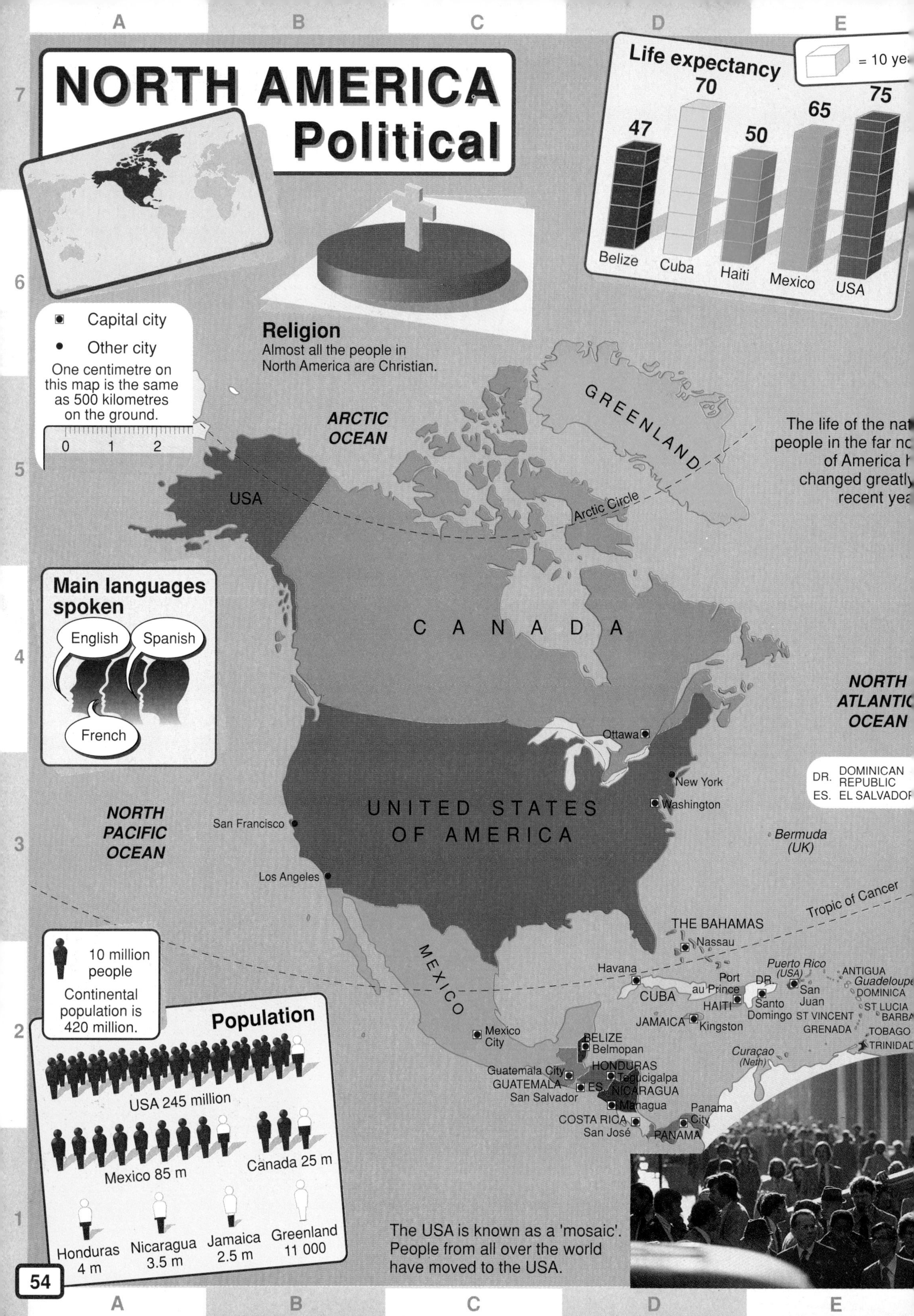
A
B
C
D
E
7
6
5
4
3
2
1
NORTH AMERICA
Political
Life expectancy
= 10 ye
47
70
50
65
75
Belize
Cuba
Haiti
Mexico
USA
Capital city
Other city
One centimetre on this map is the same as 500 kilometres on the ground.
0
1
2
Religion
Almost all the people in North America are Christian.
ARCTIC OCEAN
GREENLAND
Arctic Circle
The life of the nat
people in the far no
of America h
changed greatly
recent yea
USA
Main languages spoken
English
Spanish
French
CANADA
NORTH ATLANTIC OCEAN
Ottawa
New York
Washington
DR. DOMINICAN REPUBLIC
ES. EL SALVADOR
NORTH PACIFIC OCEAN
San Francisco
UNITED STATES OF AMERICA
Bermuda (UK)
Los Angeles
Tropic of Cancer
THE BAHAMAS
Nassau
MEXICO
10 million people
Continental population is 420 million.
Havana
Puerto Rico (USA)
ANTIGUA
Guadeloupe
Port au Prince
DR
San Juan
DOMINICA
CUBA
HAITI
Santo Domingo
ST LUCIA
ST VINCENT
BARBA
JAMAICA
Kingston
GRENADA
TOBAGO
TRINIDAD
Population
Mexico City
BELIZE
Belmopan
Curaçao (Neth)
HONDURAS
Tegucigalpa
Guatemala City
GUATEMALA
ES.
NICARAGUA
San Salvador
Managua
Panama City
COSTA RICA
San José
PANAMA
USA 245 million
Mexico 85 m
Canada 25 m
Honduras 4 m
Nicaragua 3.5 m
Jamaica 2.5 m
Greenland 11 000
The USA is known as a 'mosaic'. People from all over the world have moved to the USA.

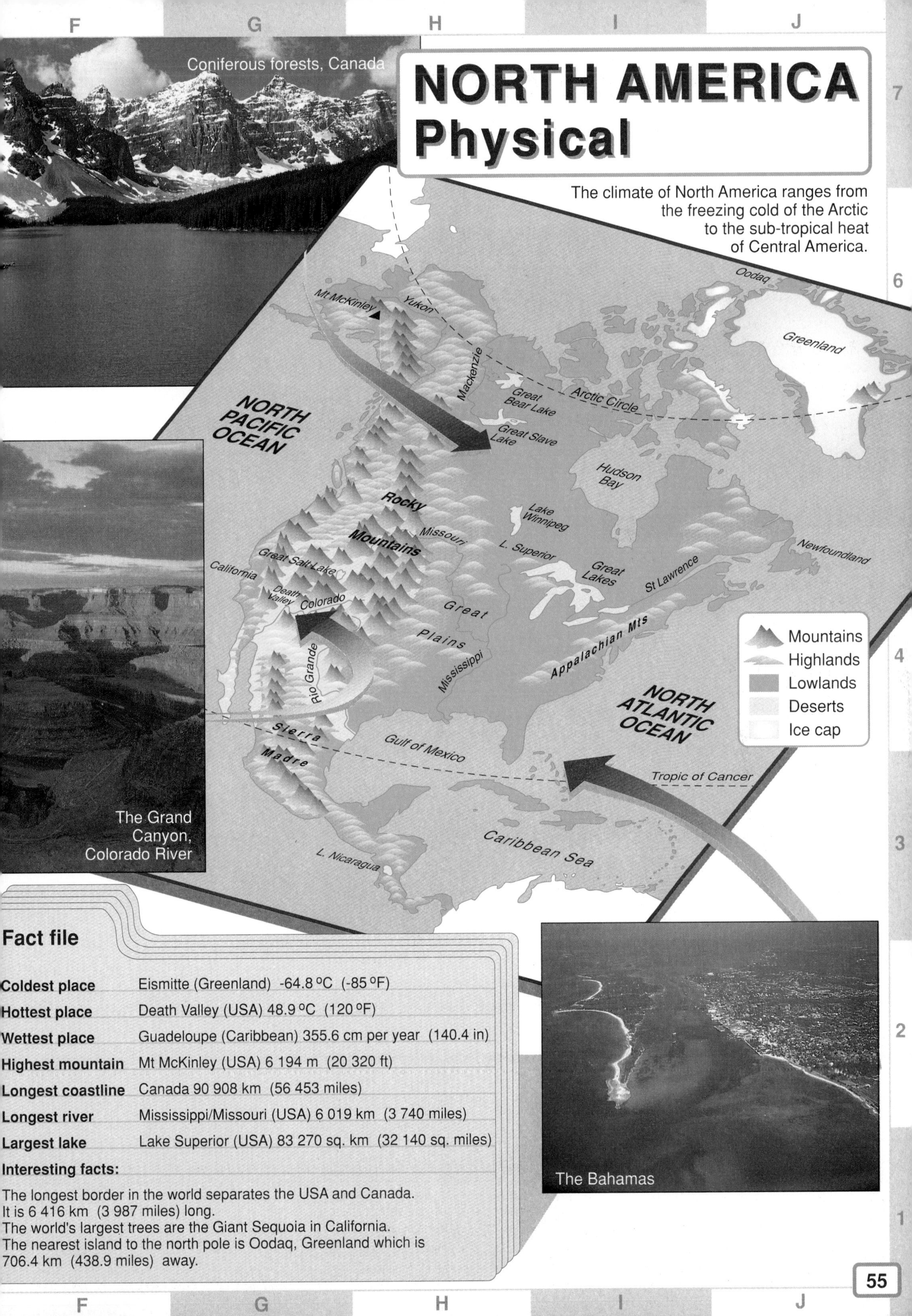
F
G
H
I
J
7
6
4
3
2
1
Mt McKinley
Yukon
Oodaq
Greenland
Mackenzie
Great Bear Lake
Arctic Circle
Great Slave Lake
NORTH PACIFIC OCEAN
Hudson Bay
Rocky Mountains
Lake Winnipeg
Missouri
L. Superior
Newfoundland
Great Salt Lake
California
Death Valley
Colorado
Great Lakes
St Lawrence
Great Plains
Appalachian Mts
Rio Grande
Mississippi
NORTH ATLANTIC OCEAN
Sierra Madre
Gulf of Mexico
Tropic of Cancer
Caribbean Sea
L. Nicaragua
Mountains
Highlands
Lowlands
Deserts
Ice cap

NORTH AMERICA Physical

The climate of North America ranges from the freezing cold of the Arctic to the sub-tropical heat of Central America.

Coniferous forests, Canada

The Grand Canyon, Colorado River

The Bahamas

Fact file

Coldest place	Eismitte (Greenland) -64.8 °C (-85 °F)
Hottest place	Death Valley (USA) 48.9 °C (120 °F)
Wettest place	Guadeloupe (Caribbean) 355.6 cm per year (140.4 in)
Highest mountain	Mt McKinley (USA) 6 194 m (20 320 ft)
Longest coastline	Canada 90 908 km (56 453 miles)
Longest river	Mississippi/Missouri (USA) 6 019 km (3 740 miles)
Largest lake	Lake Superior (USA) 83 270 sq. km (32 140 sq. miles)

Interesting facts:

The longest border in the world separates the USA and Canada. It is 6 416 km (3 987 miles) long.
The world's largest trees are the Giant Sequoia in California.
The nearest island to the north pole is Oodaq, Greenland which is 706.4 km (438.9 miles) away.

NORTH AMERICA Global Issues

Water for life

Clean water is vitally important if people are to stay healthy. Diseases carried in water kill millions of people around the world every year.

Piped water

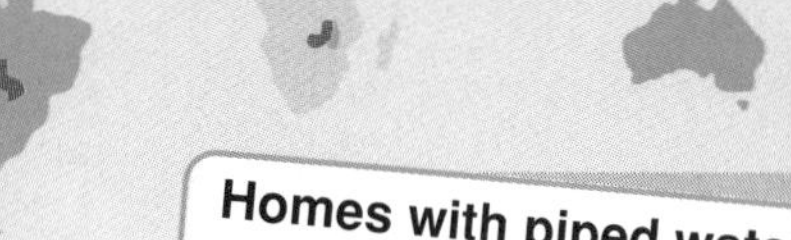

Homes with piped water

- Over 80%
- 20%-80%
- Under 20%

The danger is that as citie grow the demand for water increase and it may be impossible to provide for t needs of the people. How the use of water be reduce

Cities like Las Vegas have been built in dry parts of North America. Water for such cities has to be brought hundreds of kilometres.

Farmers require large quantities of water in order to grow crops such as grapes and cotton. This water is often taken from rivers.

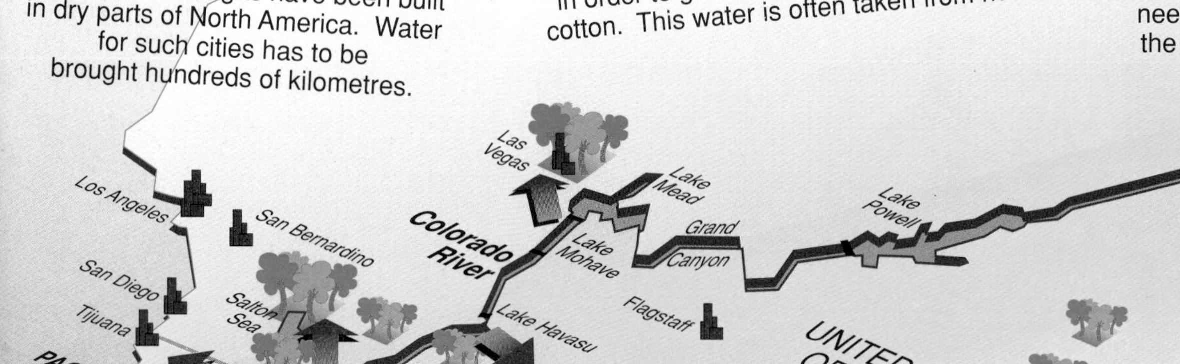

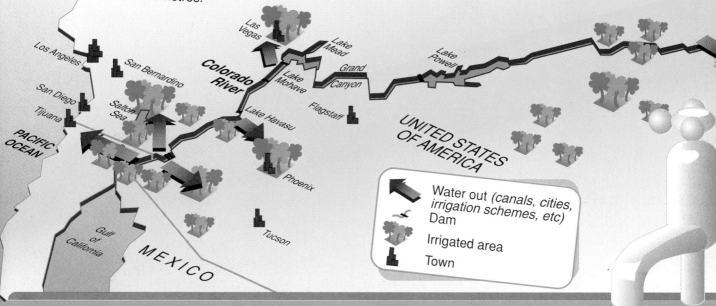

Las Vegas
Lake Mead
Lake Powell
Los Angeles
San Bernardino
Colorado River
Lake Mohave
Grand Canyon
San Diego
Salton Sea
Tijuana
Lake Havasu
Flagstaff
PACIFIC OCEAN
UNITED STATES OF AMERICA
Phoenix
Tucson
Gulf of California
MEXICO
Water out (canals, cities, irrigation schemes, etc)
Dam
Irrigated area
Town

Daily splash

Water is precious. Providing people with clean water costs money. The water has to be collected, cleaned and piped to where people live. There are very large differences in the amounts of water used by people in countries around the world. More water per person is used in North America than anywhere else.

- Afghanistan 60 litres (13 gallons)
- Thailand 80 litres (17 gallons)
- Mexico 130 litres (28 gallons)
- UK 175 litres (39 gallons)
- Russia 210 litres (46 gallons)
- USA 630 litres (140 gallons

Water consumption per person per day

Tourism

More and more people around the world are taking holidays. The number of tourists increases each year. Cheaper travel means people are going further. Many tourists now visit the islands of the Caribbean.

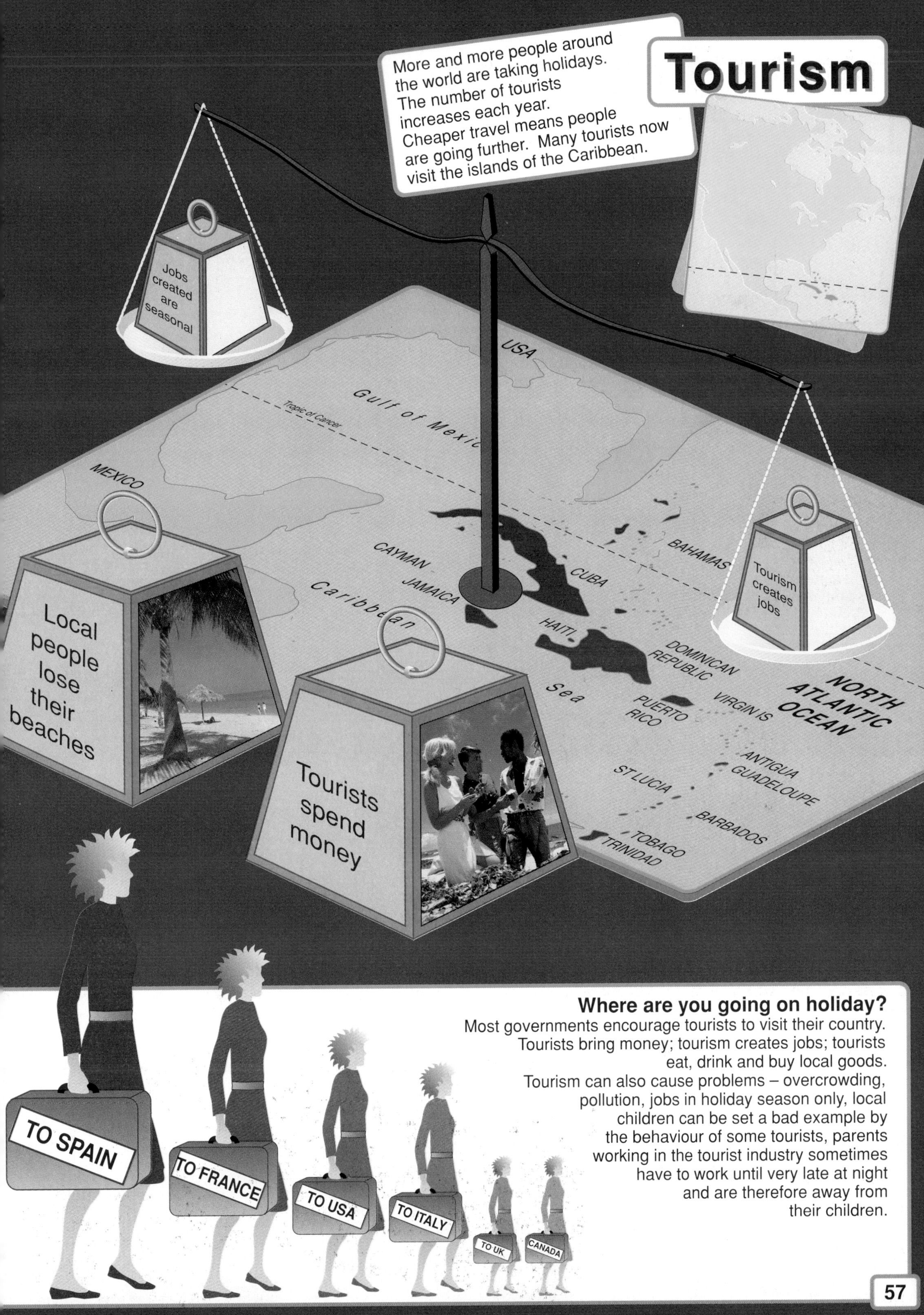

Jobs created are seasonal
Tourism creates jobs
Local people lose their beaches
Tourists spend money
USA
Gulf of Mexico
Tropic of Cancer
MEXICO
CAYMAN
JAMAICA
Caribbean Sea
CUBA
BAHAMAS
HAITI
DOMINICAN REPUBLIC
PUERTO RICO
VIRGIN IS
NORTH ATLANTIC OCEAN
ANTIGUA
GUADELOUPE
ST LUCIA
BARBADOS
TOBAGO
TRINIDAD
TO SPAIN
TO FRANCE
TO USA
TO ITALY
TO UK
CANADA

Where are you going on holiday?

Most governments encourage tourists to visit their country. Tourists bring money; tourism creates jobs; tourists eat, drink and buy local goods. Tourism can also cause problems – overcrowding, pollution, jobs in holiday season only, local children can be set a bad example by the behaviour of some tourists, parents working in the tourist industry sometimes have to work until very late at night and are therefore away from their children.

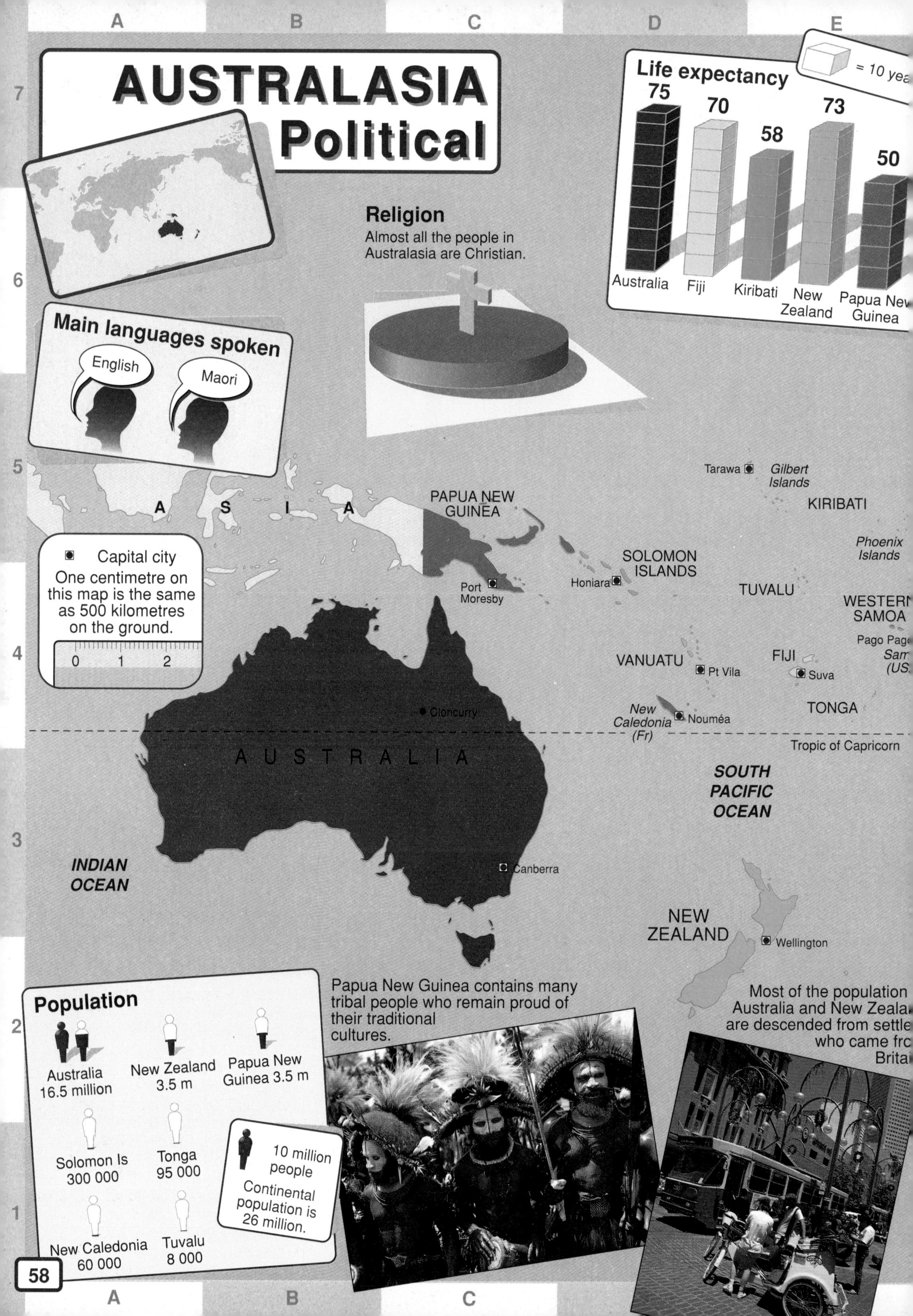

AUSTRALASIA
Political
Life expectancy
= 10 yea
75
70
58
73
50
Australia
Fiji
Kiribati
New Zealand
Papua New Guinea
Religion
Almost all the people in Australasia are Christian.
Main languages spoken
English
Maori
Capital city
One centimetre on this map is the same as 500 kilometres on the ground.
0 1 2
A S I A
PAPUA NEW GUINEA
Port Moresby
Honiara
SOLOMON ISLANDS
Tarawa
Gilbert Islands
KIRIBATI
Phoenix Islands
TUVALU
WESTERN SAMOA
Pago Pag
VANUATU
Pt Vila
FIJI
Suva
TONGA
New Caledonia (Fr)
Nouméa
Cloncurry
AUSTRALIA
Tropic of Capricorn
SOUTH PACIFIC OCEAN
INDIAN OCEAN
Canberra
NEW ZEALAND
Wellington
Population
Australia 16.5 million
New Zealand 3.5 m
Papua New Guinea 3.5 m
Solomon Is 300 000
Tonga 95 000
New Caledonia 60 000
Tuvalu 8 000
10 million people
Continental population is 26 million.
Papua New Guinea contains many tribal people who remain proud of their traditional cultures.
Most of the population Australia and New Zeala are descended from settle who came fr Brita

AUSTRALASIA Physical

H
I
J
7
6
5
3
2
1
INDIAN OCEAN
Gascoyne
Ayers Rock
Lake Eyre
Great Australian Bight
Darling
Murray
Tasmania
Mt Wilhelm
New Guinea
Great Barrier Reef
Coral Sea
PACIFIC OCEAN
Tropic of Capricorn
Tasman Sea
North Island
Lake Taupo
South Island
Mountains
Highlands
Lowlands
Deserts
F
G
H
I
J

Ayers Rock is a great tourist attraction. The Aborigines regard it as a sacred site.

The climate varies from the equatorial heat and heavy rain of Papua New Guinea to the mild climate of South Island, New Zealand with its snow-capped mountains.

Rainforest, Papua New Guinea

Southern Alps

Fact file

Coldest place	Canberra (Australia) -10°C (14°F)
Hottest place	Cloncurry (Australia) 52.8°C (127 °F)
Wettest place	Pago Pago (Samoa) 492.76 cm per year (193.6 in)
Highest mountain	Mt Wilhelm (Papua New Guinea) 4 509 m (14 793 ft)
Longest coastline	Australia 25 760 km (15 997 miles)
Longest river	Murray-Darling (Australia) 3 750 km (2 325 miles)
Largest lake	Lake Eyre (Australia) 8 900 sq. km (3 436 sq. miles)

Interesting facts:

Australasia is the smallest of the world's continents and has the lowest population.
Many of the plants and animals in Australia are not found in any other continent. This is because Australia was isolated from the other continents and its wildlife developed quite separately.

The Great Barrier Reef stretches 2 000 km along Australia's north east coast. It is one of the natural wonders of the world.
It consists of coral which is formed from the skeletons of tiny sea creatures.

ANTARCTICA

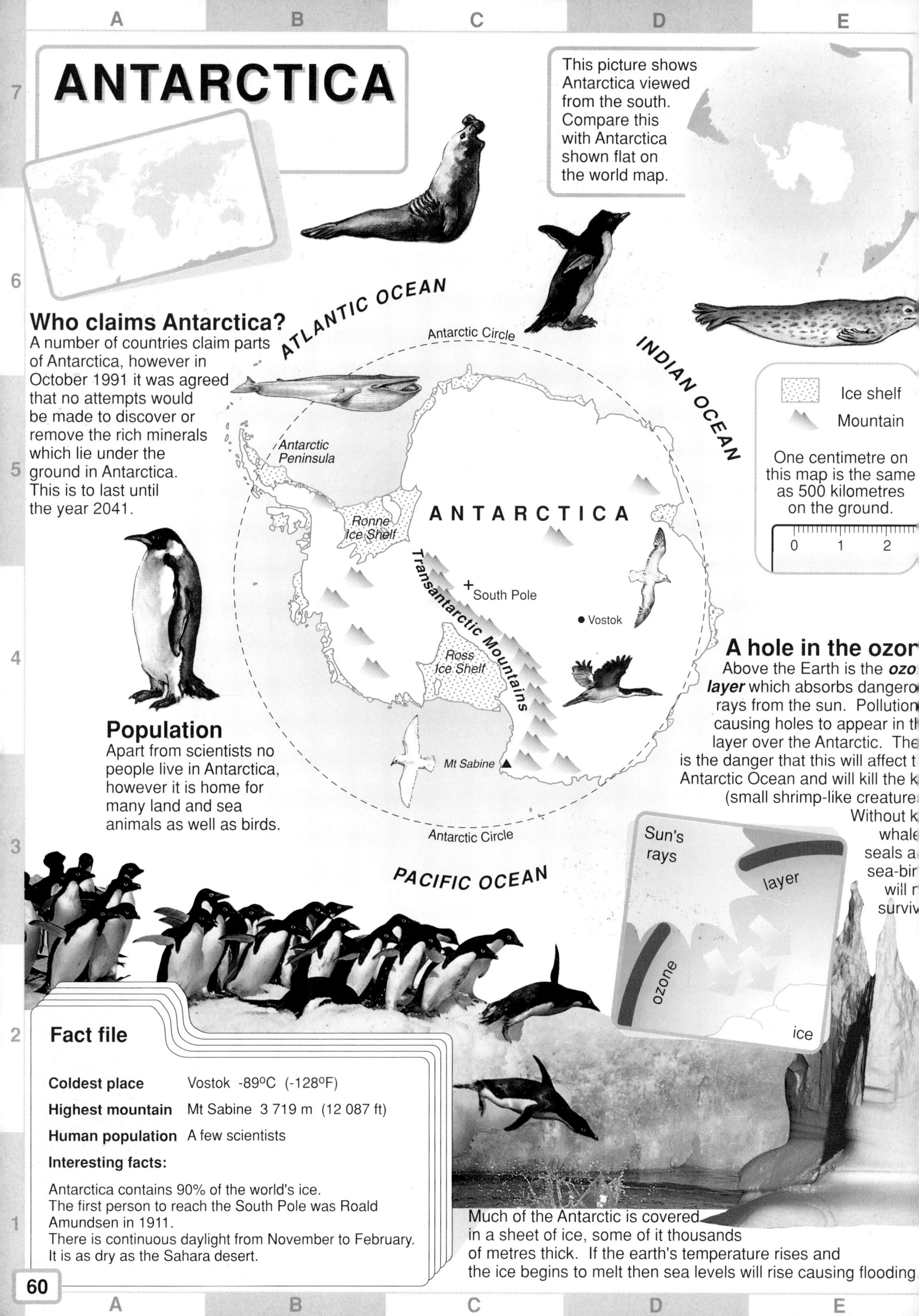

A B C D E
7 6 5 4 3 2 1
ATLANTIC OCEAN
INDIAN OCEAN
PACIFIC OCEAN
Antarctic Circle
Antarctic Peninsula
Ronne Ice Shelf
ANTARCTICA
Transantarctic Mountains
South Pole
Vostok
Ross Ice Shelf
Mt Sabine
Antarctic Circle
Ice shelf
Mountain
One centimetre on this map is the same as 500 kilometres on the ground.
0 1 2
Sun's rays
layer
ozone
ice

This picture shows Antarctica viewed from the south. Compare this with Antarctica shown flat on the world map.

Who claims Antarctica?

A number of countries claim parts of Antarctica, however in October 1991 it was agreed that no attempts would be made to discover or remove the rich minerals which lie under the ground in Antarctica. This is to last until the year 2041.

Population

Apart from scientists no people live in Antarctica, however it is home for many land and sea animals as well as birds.

A hole in the ozor

Above the Earth is the ***ozo layer*** which absorbs dangero rays from the sun. Pollution causing holes to appear in tl layer over the Antarctic. The is the danger that this will affect t Antarctic Ocean and will kill the k (small shrimp-like creature Without k whale seals a sea-bir will r surviv

Fact file

Coldest place	Vostok -89°C (-128°F)
Highest mountain	Mt Sabine 3 719 m (12 087 ft)
Human population	A few scientists

Interesting facts:

Antarctica contains 90% of the world's ice.
The first person to reach the South Pole was Roald Amundsen in 1911.
There is continuous daylight from November to February.
It is as dry as the Sahara desert.

Much of the Antarctic is covered in a sheet of ice, some of it thousands of metres thick. If the earth's temperature rises and the ice begins to melt then sea levels will rise causing flooding.

THE ARCTIC CIRCLE

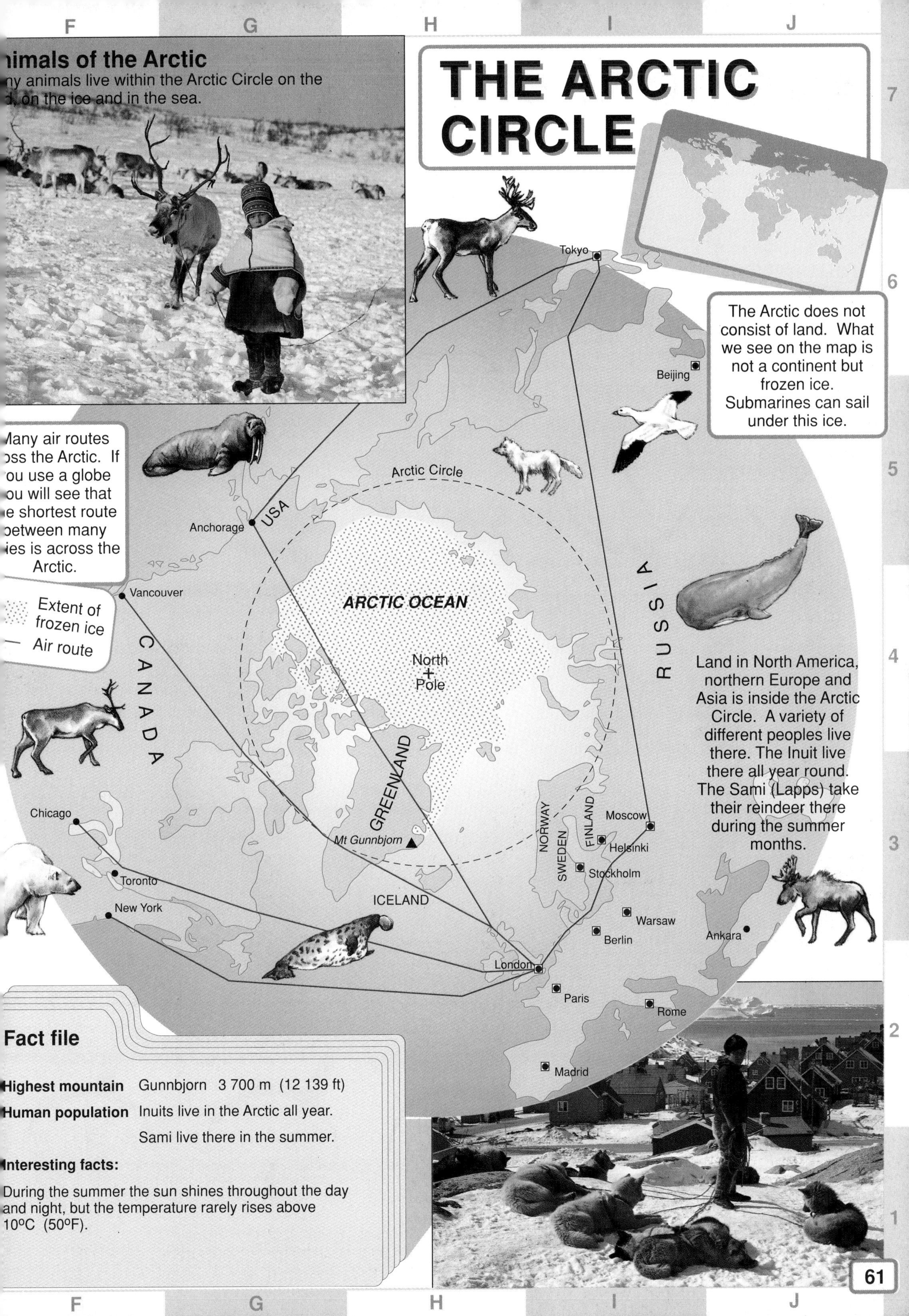

nimals of the Arctic
ny animals live within the Arctic Circle on the
d, on the ice and in the sea.
Tokyo
Beijing
Arctic Circle
Anchorage
USA
Vancouver
CANADA
ARCTIC OCEAN
North Pole
RUSSIA
GREENLAND
Mt Gunnbjorn
Chicago
Toronto
New York
ICELAND
NORWAY
SWEDEN
FINLAND
Moscow
Helsinki
Stockholm
Warsaw
Berlin
Ankara
London
Paris
Rome
Madrid
Extent of frozen ice
Air route

The Arctic does not consist of land. What we see on the map is not a continent but frozen ice. Submarines can sail under this ice.

Many air routes oss the Arctic. If ou use a globe ou will see that e shortest route between many ies is across the Arctic.

Land in North America, northern Europe and Asia is inside the Arctic Circle. A variety of different peoples live there. The Inuit live there all year round. The Sami (Lapps) take their reindeer there during the summer months.

Fact file

Highest mountain Gunnbjorn 3 700 m (12 139 ft)

Human population Inuits live in the Arctic all year.
Sami live there in the summer.

Interesting facts:

During the summer the sun shines throughout the day and night, but the temperature rarely rises above 10°C (50°F).

INTERNATIONAL TIME ZONES

Wherever we live in the world when the sun rises in the east we call it morning. When it is the middle of the day in Hong Kong it is the middle of the night in New York.

We divide the world map up into 24 zones, the same as the 24 hours in the day.

When the countries of the world agreed to a common world map showing lines of longitude the start line was drawn through Greenwich in England. At that time sailors used the world map more than anyone else and the British navy was the world's largest.

The time zones sometimes bend because some countries find it convenient to keep the same time across the whole country. Other countries like the USA, Canada, Australia and Russia have a number of time zones.

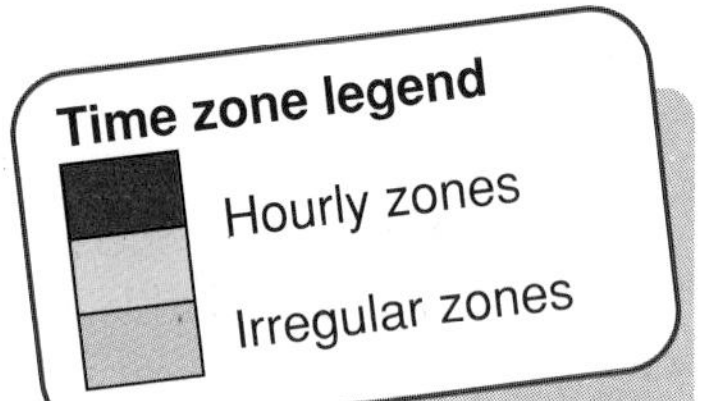
Time zone legend
Hourly zones
Irregular zones

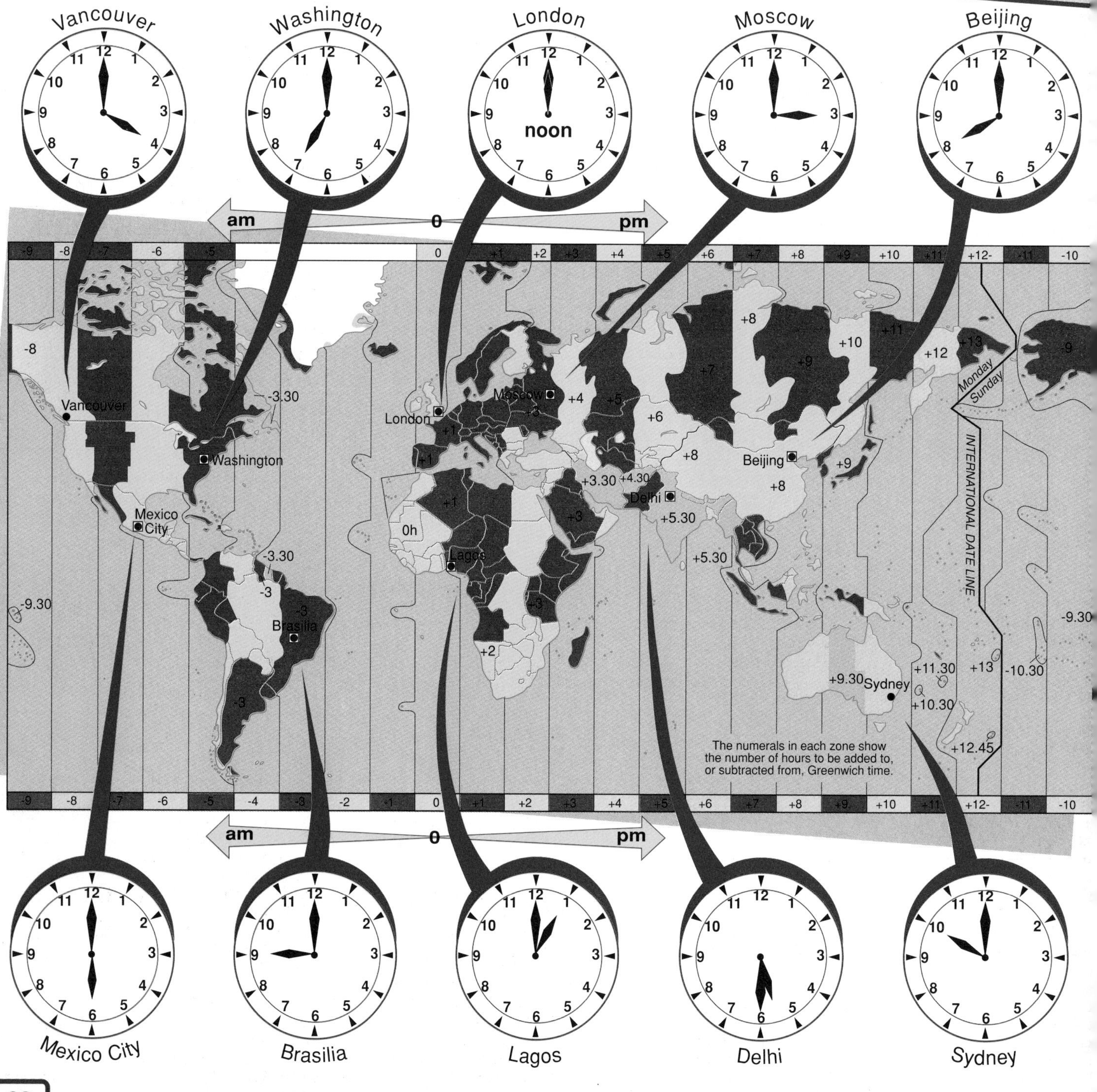

Vancouver
Washington
London
noon
Moscow
Beijing

am 0 pm

INTERNATIONAL DATE LINE
Monday
Sunday

The numerals in each zone show the number of hours to be added to, or subtracted from, Greenwich time.

am 0 pm

Mexico City
Brasilia
Lagos
Delhi
Sydney

orld index

an Ivory Coast 46 B4
Dhabi United Arab Emirates 42 D2
Ghana 46 B4
s Ababa Ethiopia 46 D4
tic Sea Europe 39 H4
an Sea Europe 39 I3
HANISTAN Asia 42 D2
a *Division* USA 35
ANIA Europe 38 E4
ian Islands North Pacific Ocean 35
ERIA Africa 46 B6
rs Algeria 46 B6
Ata Kazakhstan 42 D3
Mountains Europe 39 H4
zon *River* Brazil 51 G5
zon Basin *Feature* Brazil 51 G5
an Jordan 42 D1
erdam Netherlands 38 D3
s *Mountains* South America 51 G5
ORRA Europe 38 E2
l Falls Venezuela 51 G6
OLA Africa 46 C3
ra Turkey 42 D1
nanarivo Madagascar 46 E3
rctic Peninsula Antarctica 60 B5
rctica 60
GUA Central America 54 E2
lachian Mountains USA 55 I4
ian Desert Saudi Arabia 43 F4
ian Sea Asia 43 F4
ura Sea Australasia 37
Sea Asia 43 G5
c Ocean 61 H4
ENTINA South America 50 C3
ENIA Europe 38 E5
nsion *Island* South Atlantic Ocean 34
habad Turkmenia 42 D2
ción Paraguay 50 C4
ama Desert South America 51 G5
ns Greece 38 E4
ntic Ocean 36
s Mountains Africa 47 H6
TRALIA Australasia 58 B3
TRIA Europe 38 D3
s Rock *Feature* Australia 59 G5
RBAIJAN Europe 38 E6
es *Islands* North Atlantic Ocean 34

n Bay North America 36
hdad Iraq 42 D1
AMAS, THE North America 54 D3
Azerbaijan 38 E6
c Sea Europe 39 H5
ako Mali 46 B5
da Sea Indonesia 37
dar Seri Begawan Brunei 42 E4
gkok Thailand 42 E3
GLADESH Asia 42 D3
gui Central African Rep. 46 C4
ul The Gambia 46 A5
BADOS Central America 54 E2
of Bengal Asia 43 G4
of Biscay Europe 39 G4
ng China 42 D4
ut Lebanon 42 D1
GIUM Europe 38 D3
rade Serbia 38 E4
IZE Central America 54 D2
nopan Belize 54 D2
IN Africa 46 B4
ue *River* Nigeria 47 H5
n Germany 38 D3
nuda *Island* Atlantic Ocean 54 E3
Switzerland 38 D3
TAN Asia 42 D3
au Guinea-Bissau 46 A5

Black Sea Europe/Asia 39 I4
Bogotá Colombia 50 C6
BOLIVIA South America 50 C4
Borneo *Island* Asia 43 G3
BOSNIA HERCEGOVINA Europe 38 E3
BOTSWANA Africa 46 C3
Bouvet Island South Atlantic Ocean 34
Brahmaputra *River* Asia 43 G4
Brasilia Brazil 50 D5
BRAZIL South America 50 D5
Brazzaville Congo 46 C4
BRUNEI Asia 42 E4
Brussels Belgium 38 D3
Bucharest Romania 38 E4
Budapest Hungary 38 D4
Buenos Aires Argentina 50 C3
Bujumbura Burundi 46 D4
BULGARIA Europe 38 E4
BURKINA FASO Africa 46 B5
BURMA Asia 42 D3
BURUNDI Africa 46 D4
BYELORUSSIA Europe 38 D4

C

Cairo Egypt 46 D6
CAMBODIA Asia 42 E3
CAMEROON Africa 46 C4
CANADA North America 54 C4
Canary Islands Atlantic Ocean 47 G6
Canberra Australia 58 C3
Cape Horn South America 51 I3
Cape of Good Hope South Africa 47 G3
CAPE VERDE North Atlantic Ocean 46 A5
Caracas Venezuela 50 C6
Caribbean Sea Central America 55 H3
Caroline Islands North Pacific Ocean 35
Carpathians *Mountains* Europe 39 I4
Caspian Sea Europe/Asia 39 J4
Caucasus Mountains Europe 39 J4
Cayenne French Guiana 50 D6
Celebes Sea Asia 37
CENTRAL AFRICAN REPUBLIC Africa 46 C4
CHAD Africa 46 C5
Chatham Islands South Pacific Ocean 35
CHILE South America 50 C3
CHINA Asia 42 D3
Christmas Island Indian Ocean 35
Clipperton Island North Pacific Ocean 34
Cocos Islands Indian Ocean 35
COLOMBIA South America 50 C5
Colombo Sri Lanka 42 E3
Colorado *River* USA 55 G4
COMOROS Indian Ocean 46 E3
Conakry Guinea 46 A4
CONGO Africa 46 C4
Cook Islands South Pacific Ocean 35
Copenhagen Denmark 38 D3
Coral Sea Australasia 59 H4
COSTA RICA Central America 54 D2
Crete *Island* Greece 38 E4
CROATIA Europe 38 E3
Crozet Islands Indian Ocean 35
CUBA Central America 54 D2
Curaçao *Island* Central America 54 E2
CYPRUS Asia 42 D1
CZECHOSLOVAKIA Europe 38 D3

D

Dakar Senegal 46 A5
Damascus Syria 42 D1
Danube *River* Europe 39 H4
Dar es Salaam Tanzania 46 D4
Darling *River* Australia 59 G4
DENMARK Europe 38 D3
Dhaka Bangladesh 42 D3
DJIBOUTI Africa 46 E5
Djibouti Djibouti 46 E5
Doha Qatar 42 D2
DOMINICA Central America 54 E2
DOMINICAN REPUBLIC Central America 54 E2
Don *River* Russia 39 I4
Drakensberg *Mountains* South Africa 47 H3
Dublin Republic of Ireland 38 D2
Dushanbe Tadzhikistan 42 D2

E

East China Sea Asia 37
Easter Island South Pacific Ocean 34
ECUADOR South America 50 B5
EGYPT Africa 46 D6
El Aaiún Western Sahara 46 A5
EL SALVADOR Central America 54 D2
Elbe *River* Germany 39 H4
EQUATORIAL GUINEA Africa 46 C4
ESTONIA Europe 38 C4
ETHIOPIA Africa 46 D4
Ethiopian Highlands Ethiopia 47 J4

F

Faeroe Islands Europe 38 C2
Falkland Islands South America 50 C2
FIJI Australasia 58 E4
FINLAND Europe 38 C4
Fouta Jalon *Mountains* Guinea 47 G5
FRANCE Europe 38 D2
Franz Joseph Land *Islands* Arctic Ocean 35
Freetown Sierra Leone 46 A4
FRENCH GUIANA South America 50 D5
French Polynesia *Islands* South Pacific Ocean 35
Frunze Kirgizia 42 D2

G

GABON Africa 46 C4
Gaborone Botswana 46 D3
Galápagos Islands South Pacific Ocean 34
GAMBIA, THE Africa 46 A5
Ganges *River* India 43 G4
Gascoyne *River* Australia 59 F6
Georgetown Guyana 50 C6
GEORGIA Europe 38 E5
GERMANY Europe 38 D3
GHANA Africa 46 B4
GIBRALTAR Europe 38 E2
Gilbert Islands Kiribati 58 E5
Gobi Desert Asia 43 H4
Great Australian Bight *Bay* Australia 59 G5
Great Barrier Reef Australia 59 H5
Great Bear Lake Canada 55 H5
Great Lakes North America 55 I4
Great Plains *Feature* USA 55 H4
Great Rift Valley Africa 47 I4
Great Salt Lake USA 55 G4
Great Slave Lake Canada 55 H5
GREECE Europe 38 E4
GREENLAND North America 54 D5
Greenland Sea North America 36
GRENADA Central America 54 E2
Guadaloupe *Island* North Pacific Ocean 34
Guadeloupe *Island* Central America 54 E2
Guam *Island* North Pacific Ocean 35
GUATEMALA Central America 54 C2
Guatemala City Guatemala 54 D2
GUINEA Africa 46 A5
GUINEA-BISSAU Africa 46 A5
Gulf of Guinea Africa 47 G4
Gulf of Mexico North America 55 H4
GUYANA South America 50 C6

H

HAITI Central America 54 D2
Hanoi Vietnam 42 D4
Harare Zimbabwe 46 D3
Havana Cuba 54 D2
Hawaii *Division* USA 35
Hawaii *Island* North Pacific Ocean 35
Heard Island Indian Ocean 35
Helsinki Finland 38 C3
Himalaya *Mountains* Asia 43 G4
HONDURAS Central America 54 D2
HONG KONG Asia 42 D4
Honiara Solomon Islands 58 D4
Hudson Bay Canada 55 I5
HUNGARY Europe 38 D4

I

ICELAND Europe 38 C3
INDIA Asia 42 D3
Indian Ocean 37
INDONESIA Asia 42 E4
Indus *River* Pakistan 43 G4
IRAN Asia 42 D2
IRAQ Asia 42 D1
Ilslamabad Pakistan 42 D2
ISRAEL Asia 42 D1
ITALY Europe 38 D3
IVORY COAST Africa 46 B4

J

Jakarta Indonesia 42 E4
JAMAICA Central America 54 D2
Jan Mayen *Island* Arctic Ocean 34
JAPAN Asia 42 D5
Java Sea Indonesia 37
Johnston Atoll *Island* North Pacific Ocean 35
JORDAN Asia 42 D1
Juan Fernandez Islands South Pacific Ocean 34

K

Kabul Afghanistan 42 D2
Kalahari Desert Botswana 47 H3
Kampala Uganda 46 D4
Kathmandu Nepal 42 D3
KAZAKHSTAN Asia 42 C2
KENYA Africa 46 D4
Kerguelen Island Indian Ocean 35
Kermadec Islands South Pacific Ocean 35
Khartoum Sudan 46 D5
Kiev Ukraine 38 D4
Kigali Rwanda 46 D4
Kingston Jamaica 54 D2
Kinshasa Zaire 46 C4
KIRGIZIA Asia 42 D3
KIRIBATI Australasia 58 E5
Kishinev Moldova 38 D4
Kuala Lumpur Malaysia 42 E3
KUWAIT Asia 42 D1
Kuwait Kuwait 42 D2

L

Labrador Sea North America 36
La Paz Bolivia 50 C4
Laccadive Islands Indian Ocean 35
Lagos Nigeria 46 B4
Lake Baikal Russia 43 H4
Lake Chad Africa 47 H5
Lake Eyre Australia 59 G5
Lake Kariba Zambia/Zimbabwe 47 H3
Lake Ladoga Russia 39 H5
Lake Malawi Africa 47 I3
Lake Nicaragua Nicaragua 55 H3
Lake Superior North America 55 I5
Lake Tanganyika Africa 47 I4
Lake Taupo New Zealand 59 H3
Lake Titicaca Bolivia/Peru 51 G5
Lake Turkana Kenya 47 I4
Lake Vänern Sweden 39 H5
Lake Victoria Africa 47 I4
Lake Volta Ghana 47 G5
Lake Winnipeg Canada 55 H5
LAOS Asia 42 E3
LATVIA Europe 38 C4
LEBANON Asia 42 D1
LESOTHO Africa 46 D2
Libreville Gabon 46 C4
LIBYA Africa 46 C6
LIECHTENSTEIN Europe 38 D3
Lilongwe Malawi 46 D3
Lima Peru 50 B5
Limpopo *River* Africa 47 H3
Line Islands North Pacific Ocean 35
LIBERIA Africa 46 B4
Lisbon Portugal 38 E2

LITHUANIA Europe **38 D4**
Ljubljiana Slovenia **38 D3**
Loire *River* France **39 G4**
Lomé Togo **46 B4**
London United Kingdom **38 D2**
Los Angeles USA **54 B3**
Luanda Angola **46 C3**
Lusaka Zambia **46 D3**
LUXEMBOURG Europe **38 D3**

M

MACEDONIA Europe **38 E4**
Mackenzie *River* Canada **55 H6**
Macquarie Island South Pacific Ocean **35**
MADAGASCAR Africa **46 E3**
Madeira Islands North Atlantic Ocean **34**
Madrid Spain **38 E2**
Malabo Equatorial Guinea **46 C4**
MALAWI Africa **46 D3**
MALAYSIA Asia **42 E4**
MALDIVES Indian Ocean **35**
MALI Africa **46 B5**
Managua Nicaragua **54 D2**
Manila Philippines **42 E4**
Maputo Mozambique **46 D2**
Marcus Island North Pacific Ocean **35**
Mariana Islands North Pacific Ocean **35**
Marquesas Islands South Pacific Ocean **35**
Marshall Islands North Pacific Ocean **35**
Maseru Lesotho **46 D2**
MAURITANIA Africa **46 A5**
MAURITIUS Indian Ocean **46 E3**
Mbabane Swaziland **46 D2**
Mediterranean Sea Europe/Africa **39 I3**
Mekong *River* Asia **43 G3**
MEXICO Central America **54 C3**
Mexico City Mexico **54 C2**
Midway Islands North Pacific Ocean **35**
Minsk Byelorussia **38 D4**
Mississippi *River* USA **55 H4**
Missouri *River* USA **55 H5**
Mogadishu Somalia **46 E4**
MOLDOVA Europe **38 D4**
MONGOLIA Asia **42 C3**
Monrovia Liberia **46 A4**
MONTENEGRO Europe **38 E4**
Montevideo Uruguay **50 D3**
MOROCCO Africa **46 B6**
Moscow Russia **38 D5**
Mount Aconcagua Argentina **51 H4**
Mount Cameroon Cameroon **47 H4**
Mount Elbrus Russia **39 J4**
Mount Everest Asia **43 G4**
Mount Gunnbjorn Greenland **61 H3**
Mount Kenya Kenya **47 I4**
Mount Kilimanjaro Tanzania **47 I4**
Mount McKinley USA **55 H6**
Mount Sabine Antarctica **60 C3**
Mount Toubkal Morocco **47 H6**
Mount Wilhelm Papua New Guinea **59 I5**
MOZAMBIQUE Africa **46 D3**
Murray *River* Australia **59 G4**
Muscat Oman **42 D2**

N

Nairobi Kenya **46 D4**
Namib Desert Namibia **47 G3**
NAMIBIA Africa **46 C3**
Nassau The Bahamas **54 D2**
Ndjaména Chad **46 C5**
NEPAL Asia **42 D3**
NETHERLANDS Europe **38 D3**
New Caledonia *Islands* Australasia **58 D4**
New Delhi India **42 D3**
New Guinea *Island* Australasia **59 H5**
New York USA **54 D3**
NEW ZEALAND Australąsia **58 D2**
Newfoundland *Island* Canada **55 J5**
Niamey Niger **46 B5**
NICARAGUA Central America **54 D2**
Nicosia Cyprus **42 D1**
NIGER Africa **46 C5**
Niger *River* Africa **47 H5**
NIGERIA Africa **46 C4**
Nile *River* Africa **47 J4**
Niue Island South Pacific Ocean **35**
North Atlantic Ocean 36
North Island New Zealand **59 H3**
NORTH KOREA Asia **42 D4**
North Pacific Ocean 37
North Sea Europe **39 G4**
NORWAY Europe **38 C3**
Norwegian Sea Europe **39 G5**
Nouakchott Mauritania **46 A5**
Nouméa New Caledonia **58 D4**
Nubian Desert Sudan **47 J5**

O

OMAN Asia **42 D2**
Orange *River* South Africa **47 G3**
Orinoco *River* Venezuela **51 F6**
Oslo Norway **38 C3**
Ottawa Canada **54 D4**
Ouagadougou Burkina Faso **46 B5**

P

Pacific Ocean 37
Pago Pago Samoa **58 E4**
PAKISTAN Asia **42 D2**
Pampas *Feature* Argentina **51 H4**
PANAMA Central America **54 D1**
Panama City Panama **54 D2**
PAPUA NEW GUINEA Australasia **58 C5**
PARAGUAY South America **50 C4**
Paraguay *River* Argentina **51 H5**
Paramaribo Surinam **50 D6**
Paraná *River* South America **51 H5**
Paris France **38 D2**
Persian Gulf Asia **43 F4**
PERU South America **50 B5**
Philippine Sea Asia **43 H3**
PHILIPPINES Asia **42 E4**
Phnom Penh Cambodia **42 E3**
Phoenix Islands Kiribati **58 E5**
Pitcairn Island South Pacific Ocean **34**
Po *River* Italy **39 H4**
Podgorica Montenegro **38 E4**
POLAND Europe **38 D4**
Port au Prince Haiti **54 D2**
Port Moresby Papua New Guinea **58 C4**
Port Vila Vanuatu **58 D4**
Porto Novo Benin **46 B4**
PORTUGAL Europe **38 E2**
Prague Czechoslovakia **38 D3**
Pretoria South Africa **46 D2**
Prince Edward Islands
South Atlantic Ocean **34**
Puerto Rico *Island* Central America **54 E2**
Pyongyang North Korea **42 D4**
Pyrenees *Mountains* France/Spain **39 H3**

Q

QATAR Asia **42 D2**
Quito Ecuador **50 B5**

R

Rabat Morocco **46 B6**
Rangoon Burma **42 E3**
Red Sea Africa/Asia **47 J5**
REPUBLIC OF IRELAND Europe **38 D2**
Réunion *Island* Indian Ocean **46 E3**
Revilla Gigedo Islands
North Pacific Ocean **34**
Reykjavik Iceland **38 C1**
Rhine *River* Europe **39 H4**
Rhône *River* France **39 H4**
Riga Latvia **38 C4**
Rio de Janiero Brazil **50 D5**
Rio Grande *River* North America **55 G4**
River Plate South America **51 I4**
Riyadh Saudi Arabia **42 D1**
Rocky Mountains North America **55 H5**
ROMANIA Europe **38 D4**
Rome Italy **38 D3**
Ronne Ice Shelf Antarctica **60 B5**
Ross Ice Shelf Antarctica **60 C4**
RUSSIA Europe **38 C5**
RUSSIA Asia **42 B4**
Ruwenzori Range *Mountains*
Uganda/Zaire **47 I4**
RWANDA Africa **46 D4**

S

Sahara *Desert* Africa **47 H6**
Samoa *Islands* Australasia **58 E4**
San Ambrosio *Island* South
Pacific Ocean **34**
San Francisco USA **54 B3**
San José Costa Rica **54 D2**
San Juan Puerto Rico **54 E2**
San Salvador El Salvador **54 D2**
San'a Yemen **42 E1**
Santiago Chile **50 C3**
Santo Domingo Dominican Republic **54 E2**
São Paulo Brazil **50 D5**
SÃO TOME AND PRINCIPE Africa **46 C4**
Sarajevo Bosnia Hercegovina **38 E4**
SAUDI ARABIA Asia **42 D1**
Scotia Sea South America **36**
Sea of Japan Asia **43 H4**
Sea of Okhotsk Russia **37**
SENEGAL Africa **46 A5**
Seoul South Korea **42 D4**
SERBIA Europe **38 E4**
SEYCHELLES Indian Ocean **46 E4**
Shannon *River* Republic of Ireland **39 G4**
Siberia *Feature* Russia **43 H5**
SIERRA LEONE Africa **46 A4**
Sierra Madre *Mountains* Mexico **55 G4**
Singapore Singapore **42 E3**
SINGAPORE Asia **42 E3**
Skopje Macedonia **38 E4**
SLOVENIA Europe **38 E3**
Socotra Indian Ocean **35**
Sofia Bulgaria **38 E4**
SOLOMON ISLANDS Australasia **58 D4**
SOMALIA Africa **46 E4**
SOUTH AFRICA Africa **46 C2**
South Atlantic Ocean 36
South China Sea Asia **43 G4**
South Georgia *Island*
South Atlantic Ocean **34**
South Island New Zealand **59 H3**
SOUTH KOREA Asia **42 D4**
South Pacific Ocean 36
South Sandwich Islands
South Atlantic Ocean **34**
SPAIN Europe **38 E2**
SRI LANKA Asia **42 E3**
St. Helena *Island* South Atlantic
Ocean **34**
St. Lawrence *River* North America **55 I4**
ST. LUCIA Central America **54 E2**
St. Paul Island Indian Ocean **35**
ST. VINCENT Central America **54 E2**
Steppes *Feature* Asia **43 G5**
Stockholm Sweden **38 C3**
SUDAN Africa **46 D5**
Sumatera *Island* Indonesia **43 G3**
SURINAM South America **50 D5**
Suva Fiji **58 E4**
Svalbard Islands Arctic Ocean **34**
SWAZILAND Africa **46 D2**
SWEDEN Europe **38 C3**
SWITZERLAND Europe **38 D3**
SYRIA Asia **42 D1**

T

TADZHIKISTAN Asia **42 D2**
Tagus *River* Portugal **39 G3**
Taipei Taiwan **42 D4**
TAIWAN Asia **42 D4**
Tallinn Estonia **38 C4**
TANZANIA Africa **46 D3**
Tarawa Kiribati **58 E5**
Tashkent Uzbekistan **42 D2**
Tasman Sea Australasia **59 H4**
Tasmania *Island* Australia **59 G4**
Tbilisi Georgia **38 E5**
Tegucigalpa Honduras **54 D2**
Tehran Iran **42 D2**
Tel Aviv Israel **42 D1**
THAILAND Asia **42 E3**
Thames *River* UK **39 G4**
Thimphu Bhutan **42 D3**
Tian Shan *Mountains* Asia **43 G4**
Tibesti Massif *Mountains* Africa **47**
Tirana Albania **38 E4**
Tobago *Island* Central America **54 E**
TOGO Africa **46 B4**
Tokelau Islands Pacific Ocean **35**
Tokyo Japan **42 D5**
TONGA Australasia **58 E4**
Transantarctic
Mountains Antarctica **60 C4**
Trinidad *Island* Central America **54 E**
TRINIDAD AND TOBAGO
Central America **54 E2**
Tripoli Libya **46 C6**
Tristan da Cunha *Island*
South Atlantic Ocean **34**
Tuamotu Archipelago *Islands*
South Pacific Ocean **35**
Tunis Tunisia **46 C6**
TUNISIA Africa **46 C6**
TURKEY Asia **42 D1**
TURKMENIA Asia **42 D2**
TUVALU Australasia **58 E4**

U

UGANDA Africa **46 D4**
UKRAINE Europe **38 D4**
Ulan Bator Mongolia **42 C4**
UNITED ARAB EMIRATES Asia **42**
UNITED KINGDOM Europe **38 D2**
UNITED STATES OF AMERICA
North America **54 C3**
Urals *Mountains* Europe **39 J5**
URUGUAY South America **50 C3**
UZBEKISTAN Asia **42 D2**

V

VANUATU Australasia **58 D4**
VENEZUELA South America **50 C6**
Vienna Austria **38 D3**
Vientiane Laos **42 D3**
VIETNAM Asia **42 E4**
Vilnius Lithuania **38 D4**
Vladivostok Russia **42 D4**
Volga *River* Russia **39 I5**

W

Wake Island North Pacific Ocean **35**
Warsaw Poland **38 D4**
Washington USA **54 D3**
Wellington New Zealand **58 E2**
WESTERN SAHARA Africa **46 A5**
WESTERN SAMOA Australasia **58 E**
Windhoek Namibia **46 C3**

Y

Yangtze *River* China **43 H4**
Yaoundé Cameroon **46 C4**
Yellow Sea Asia **37**
YEMEN Asia **42 E1**
Yerevan Armenia **38 E5**
YUGOSLAVIA Europe **38 E4**
Yukon *River* North America **55 H6**

Z

Zagreb Croatia **38 D3**
ZAIRE Africa **46 C4**
Zaire *River* Zaire **47 H4**
Zaire Basin *Feature* Zaire **47 H4**
Zambezi *River* Africa **47 H3**
ZAMBIA Africa **46 D3**
ZIMBABWE Africa **46 D3**